Creating Your High School Resume

Creating Your High School Resume

A Step-by-Step Guide to Preparing an Effective Resume for College and Career

Kathryn Kraemer Troutman

Indianapolis, IN

Creating Your High School Resume

A Step-by-Step Guide to Preparing an Effective Resume for College and Career

© 1998 by Kathryn Kraemer Troutman

Published by JIST Works, an imprint of JIST Publishing, Inc.
8902 Otis Avenue
Indianapolis, IN 46216
Phone: 1-800-648-JIST Fax: 1-800-JIST-FAX E-mail: info@jist.com
World Wide Web Address: http://www.jist.com. Visit our Web site for information about other JIST products.

Cover Design by Michael Nolan

Printed in the United States of America.

05 04 03 02   9 8 7 6 5 4

We have been careful to provide accurate information throughout this book, but it is possible that errors and omissions have been introduced. Please consider this in making any career plans or other important decisions. Trust your own judgment above all else and in all things.

The resume samples and photos in this workbook have been used with permission of students. Names and other information have been changed to protect privacy.

ISBN 1-56370-508-7

Preface

If you are like most high school students, you probably have not given much thought to preparing your resume. Resumes are for parents, teachers, and professional people with careers, right? Wrong! A resume is your ticket to finding part-time, summer, and full-time work, applying for internships and college, and ultimately achieving your goals.

Creating Your High School Resume takes you step-by-step through the resume-writing process. Do you have an idea of what you'd like to do in your future career? Are you interested in a certain field already? Are you college bound? Do you have special skills or abilities (for example, in computers, music, child care, or writing)?

This book shows you how to put all these details plus a lot more into your resume. Your resume is one of the most important career documents you are going to write—over and over again—for the next several decades. It's true. Most professionals update their resumes regularly and refocus their resumes to appeal to a potential employer's needs.

Your resume is an opportunity to reflect your energy and interest in life. Are you active in school clubs or teams? Do you have awards or accomplishments of which you are proud? These activities are important in developing skills, meeting people, and gaining experience. I help you describe this information on your resume.

This book will show that you

- Can be a great student, volunteer, and employee

- Possess skills and abilities already

- Are a loyal person and hard worker

- Can be an asset on any team

How This Book Is Organized

Chapter 1 introduces you to reasons for writing your resume now. Chapter 2 explains the types of resumes and which one is right for you. Directions for writing the various sections of your resume are given in Chapters 3 and 4. You put your resume into an attractive format in Chapter 5.

In Chapter 6, you learn how to put a complete package together with cover letters, reference lists, and thank-you letters. Chapter 7 shows examples of real student resumes for inspiration and ideas. Finally, Chapter 8 provides guidance for a successful job search.

Activities are indicated with a "To Do" headline throughout the book. A continuing case study of one student shows you how her resume changed with her career focus. Information on using the Web and e-mail effectively is scattered throughout the text. Tips highlight suggestions to make your resume writing easier.

With a wealth of encouragement, advice, and examples, *Creating Your High School Resume* will make writing your first resume a thought-provoking and successful experience. Good luck!

Table of Contents

Chapter 8:
Job Search Tips — 117

Index — 133

Acknowledgments

The literature that addresses high school students' transition to professional life is scarce. When found, this information often is out-of-sync with contemporary trends.

For this reason, I extend special acknowledgment to the students at Catonsville High School, Western School of Technology, and elsewhere, who generously shared their resumes and lives with me. In this way, they have helped the career education of an eager and promising generation. Their enthusiasm and unaffected desire to learn, move, and succeed have been my source of rejuvenation throughout the tedious editing and production process.

My grateful acknowledgments must also go to this book's editors (who surely feel as much stake in it as I do): Bonny Kraemer, my sister and Resume Place manager; Jeff McDaniel, Catonsville High School English teacher; and Susan Pines, the JIST Works editor who reshaped the book into what it is today. Many thanks also to the following JIST staff: associate publisher Marta Partington, senior editor David Noble, and graphic designer Aleata Howard.

Through continuing academic and professional camaraderie, Cindy Cairns, Patricia Brown, and Sally McNabb have graciously shown me the need for a book like this in high schools. Many thanks.

Special thanks to professional resume writers Gayle Bernstein and Kathlene Y. McNamee for their contributions to this book.* Gayle, in addition to high school counselor Bonny Hannigan, reviewed this book for content and accuracy. My thanks to you.

Finally, I send loving praise to my three children. Thanks, in particular, to my daughter for her unique and timely contribution to the book. My children are my inspiration and motivation and the voice of all young adults in their quest for a place in society.

* Below is contact information for contributing professional resume writers. Both possess CPRW certification, for Certified Professional Résumé Writer.

Gayle Bernstein, CPRW
Typing PLUS
2710 East 62nd Street
Indianapolis, IN 46220
Phone (317) 257-6789
Fax (317) 479-3103

Kathlene Y. McNamee, CPRW
The Word Wizard
523 E. Front St.
Butte, MT 59701
Phone/Fax: (406) 782-1063

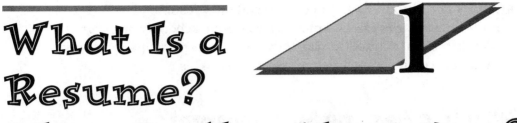

What Is a Resume? Why Do You Need One?

Exactly where does this fit into my career path?

This chapter introduces you to the definitions of a resume and the reasons why developing and maintaining a resume are so important. You will learn that a resume can help open your mind to your potential and open the door to future opportunities.

Definitions of a Resume

Here are two definitions of a resume. The first is from a dictionary. The second is the author's definition, written to fit your situation as a high school student.

Webster's definition of a resume: Summary. Specifically, a short account of one's career and qualifications prepared typically by an applicant for a position.

Author's definition of a high school student's resume: One 8 ½ x 11 sheet that summarizes and emphasizes your high school courses, grades, academic honors, extracurricular activities, sports participation, work experience, volunteer experience, and special skills.

Why Is a Resume So Important?

The resume you write in high school is important because it is probably your first resume. Developing information about yourself into a resume helps you do the following:

- ✉ Organize your thoughts

- ✉ Recognize your skills and interests

- ✉ Make more educated college and career choices

- ✉ Ultimately achieve your goals

- ✉ Most importantly, feel good about yourself and your accomplishments

As you create your resume, you will think about what you've accomplished and where your interests lie. After you've created your first resume, this thinking process will continue and help you make choices about your future education, training, and occupation.

> **TIP** YOU MAY UPDATE YOUR RESUME AS OFTEN AS EVERY SIX MONTHS THROUGHOUT HIGH SCHOOL, AS YOU GAIN EXPERIENCES TO WRITE ABOUT AND CHANGE YOUR INTERESTS OR GOALS.

Discovering what you want to do for a career is a challenge. Your first resume can open doors to opportunities that will help you decide what field interests you most right now. The resume is your tool to introduce yourself and promote your involvement in a work or educational opportunity.

When you begin college or your career, you may use your resume often for jobs, introductions, and continuing education. Both now and later, you will feel good about yourself when you see on one sheet all that you have accomplished. It's your record of skills and achievements documented on paper, ready and available to share with anyone who can help or hire you.

Your Resume Will Grow and Change with Your Activities and Interests

Your activities in high school are important for your first resume. These activities help you become aware of your interests and natural abilities. These activities also can help you recognize your career potential.

Are you still uncertain how activities such as playing shortstop, practicing the piano, or taking part in the school play can affect your resume and your future? Consider the following examples:

- A high school athlete may become a sportscaster, physical education teacher, or physical therapist.

- A student active in band and orchestra may become a professional musician, composer, music educator, or music therapist.

- A student interested in theater, debate, or school leadership positions may have promise in a teaching, business, or political career.

In addition, your interests outside of school, such as caring for cars, kids, or computers, may lead you to pursue paid or volunteer work. This work experience will strengthen your resume and help you decide if a field interests you as a college major or a future career. Realizing that a certain field is *not* for you is as helpful as realizing that another one *is*.

If you change your mind about a field, you can change your resume as well. For example, right now you may want to be an automotive or aircraft mechanic, so you may participate in tech prep courses and internships. Your resume will reflect your goals and accomplishments at this point. Later, you may decide to pursue a construction management career. You will want your resume to mirror your new interests. On your updated resume, therefore, you will emphasize math and computer-aided design courses and any construction experience you can get. You will probably change ideas about your career direction many times before—and after—you graduate!

TIP ASK YOUR LIBRARIAN FOR BOOKS AND PUBLICATIONS THAT CAN HELP YOU RESEARCH FIELDS AND CAREERS.

Follow the Changing Resume of a Real Student

Emily Thompson

In this book, you will see various versions of Emily Thompson's resume. You will look at her resume as a junior, when she was interested in writing, public policy, and education. Then you will view her resumes as a senior, when training and internships turned her focus to writing and environmental science. You also will see Emily's college resume, which includes everything important for her continuing education.

As you read Emily's case study, note how her resume grew and changed based on her evolving interests and career goals. Her resume is written in several ways, and you will learn the rationale behind the various presentations.

TIP YOUR INTERESTS, EXPERIENCES, AND GRADES ARE SURE TO BE DIFFERENT FROM EMILY'S. MANY OTHER EXAMPLES APPEAR IN THIS BOOK TO HELP YOU RECOGNIZE YOUR SKILLS AND MAKE THE MOST OF WHAT YOU'VE DONE. THESE EXAMPLES HELP YOU THINK ABOUT WHAT YOU CAN DO TO GET GREAT EXPERIENCE AND GOOD RESUME MATERIAL.

You might be wondering what the difference is between a high school student's resume and a professional person's resume? The main difference is the amount of time and information it covers—the format may be quite similar. For example, you've been in high school two to four years, but an adult may have been out of high school for five to twenty years (or more!).

So, make the best of what you have. As you achieve new goals, you will start to take old information off your resume. Until then, include every important experience you can.

What Can a Resume Do for You? When Can You Use It?

Resumes serve numerous practical purposes. The rest of this chapter explains the main ways you will use your resume.

Applying for Jobs

A good resume makes looking for work much easier. Many employers won't consider you without a resume and will be impressed if you have one at such a young age. Consider the following three situations:

⊠ **Applying for summer and part-time openings.** For job consideration, send or drop off your resume and cover letter. (Cover letter samples appear in Chapter 6.) You may be responding to classified ads or contacting a business that you know hires students. If you see a classified ad in your local or city newspaper that looks interesting, send your resume in the mail with a cover letter informing the company or individual of your interest and availability.

If you heard about an opening through someone you know or have spoken with a potential employer before sending the resume, mention this in your cover letter. You'll have an edge over other applicants. (See Chapter 8 for job-hunting tips.)

> **TIP** MANY COMPANIES HAVE A WEB SITE, AND SOME LIST JOB OPENINGS ON THE WEB! YOU CAN CONTACT A COMPANY ELECTRONICALLY IF ITS WEB PAGE LISTS E-MAIL AS AN ACCEPTABLE WAY TO APPLY. IF THE COMPANY ALLOWS IT, SEND YOUR RESUME THROUGH E-MAIL, EITHER AS AN ATTACHED FILE (IF YOU KNOW YOUR WORD PROCESSORS ARE COMPATIBLE) OR IN THE TEXT BOX. A WEB RESUME IS ANOTHER OPTION AND CAN BE REALLY COOL WITH SCANNED-IN PHOTOS, EXAMPLES OF YOUR WRITING OR PROJECTS, AND TEACHERS' RECOMMENDATIONS. CHECK OUT WWW.RESUME-PLACE.COM TO SEE THE WEB RESUME OF EMILY THOMPSON, THIS BOOK'S ONGOING CASE STUDY STUDENT. YOU WILL BE INSPIRED!

⊠ **Using a resume in addition to a job application.** Even if a company uses job applications, attach your resume to the application. Job applications may have limited space or may not include sections for all the information you want to convey. Attaching your resume to applications gives potential employers a better description of your talents and how you may help their businesses. You may find that some employers require both a job application and a resume.

⊠ **Approaching a business owner for a job.** If you walk in the door of a potential employer and ask for work, you most likely will not get an interview. An employee probably will reply, "I don't know if we are hiring. The manager's not here." You can then say, "May I leave my resume so that if you are hiring now or in the future, your manager can call me? I am available 15 hours per week, and evenings are okay." This shows the employer that you are highly prepared and professional.

Another job search technique is to look in the yellow pages for companies that interest you. Call the manager and express your interest in the company. Follow up with a resume and ask for an interview. This may be a bit scary at first. But you may find out about a job opening before it's publicized!

 TIP A RESUME ALONE USUALLY WON'T GET YOU HIRED, BUT IT IS OFTEN NECESSARY TO PROVIDE ONE TO EMPLOYERS. WITHOUT A RESUME, YOU MAY NOT GET CONSIDERED AT ALL.

To Do:

Look at the employment ads in your local newspaper. Read them from beginning to end and cut out any jobs that interest you (as if you were looking for a job right now). Paste them here. If you were in the job market, you could send your resume and cover letter to apply for these positions.

Paste ad here	Paste ad here

Applying to Colleges

Applying for college is a huge project. Each college requires a personal statement and a separate application with sections for activities, skills, and experience. If you have your resume on hand, you can refer to it when completing applications. A resume also can help you compose your personal statement by reminding you of school and extracurricular activities that are relevant to your educational goals. Including the resume with your package can help admissions representatives understand your background.

Applying for Scholarships

Many scholarship applications request work samples, personal statements, letters, and other information. You can also enclose your resume, which is a total presentation of your education and experience, for the scholarship committee members. It will save them time, create a good impression, and help them make a decision about the scholarship.

Looking for Internships

An *internship* is a job, sometimes with pay and sometimes without, that helps you learn a specific task and gives you exposure to an industry. For an internship position, the organization where you work usually trains you and spends extra time with you. Internships are sometimes incredibly competitive and desirable. You need to apply for an internship with a resume and cover letter, the same process that you go through when applying for a job.

In your resume for an internship, you should convey sincerity, dependability, qualifications, and interest in an organization and give reasons for applying. You must show that you are worthy of a company's time and training.

Finding Mentors

A *mentor* is a professional person who is successful and has experience in a specific field. A mentor is someone who has time to talk to you occasionally about what it's like to work in an occupation. This person will give you ideas about training, courses, and specialized skills that you need in order to succeed in an industry. Your mentor might refer you to hiring managers of companies, if the mentor thinks you are qualified and have potential.

The following are examples of career fields and mentors:

CAREER FIELD	MENTOR
Fashion/Retailing	Store manager/Buyer
Sports management	Arena or team manager
Writing	Journalist
Web site development	Webmaster
Space science	NASA employee
Veterinary medicine	Veterinarian/Veterinary technician
Sales and Marketing	Sales manager/Sales executive/Advertising executive
Small business	Store owner/Small business owner

The way to find a mentor is to research the field, looking for the name of someone in your city or town who might be able to help you start exploring a career. Then write a letter and send your resume. Ask if the individual has time to be a mentor to a young person aspiring to work in the same field.

TIP NEWSPAPERS, PUBLICATIONS ABOUT SPECIFIC INDUSTRIES, AND COMPANY WEB SITES MAY CONTAIN POTENTIAL MENTORS' NAMES. SOME NEWSPAPERS LIST PROFESSIONALS WHO HAVE BEEN PROMOTED OR NEWLY HIRED. WRITE TO ONE OF THESE PEOPLE AND SAY, "CONGRATULATIONS ON YOUR NEW JOB. I KNOW YOU'RE BUSY, BUT COULD YOU TAKE A FEW MINUTES TO TELL ME HOW YOU GOT TO YOUR CURRENT CAREER? I'M A HIGH SCHOOL STUDENT WHO ASPIRES TO BE A FINANCIAL MANAGER." THE INDIVIDUAL MAY CONSENT TO GIVE YOU 15 MINUTES, WHICH COULD TURN INTO A STUDENT-MENTOR SITUATION IF YOU SHOW INTEREST AND PROMISE.

To Do:

Name someone to whom you could send your resume and whom you could ask to be your mentor. What is his or her job title, company name, telephone number, and address?

_____

_____

_____

_____

_____

Describe what you want to learn from this person.

_____

_____

_____

_____

_____

Getting References

A *reference* is someone who has known you for some time and will recommend you to an employer. A teacher, school counselor, community leader, and minister may make good references. Former supervisors are usually the best references after you are in the workforce.

You can send your resume with a letter to your references, so that they know you are searching for a position or applying for college. If your references receive a call from an interested organization, they will be more familiar with your total accomplishments. It's possible that they do not know all your activities or honors. People who serve as your references can do a better job of stating your strengths if they have your resume nearby. Individuals like to give complete, knowledgeable references.

TIP BE SURE TO ASK PEOPLE IF THEY WOULD BE YOUR REFERENCE *BEFORE* YOU GIVE THEIR NAMES TO POTENTIAL EMPLOYERS OR COLLEGES. TELL REFERENCES ABOUT YOUR PLANS SO THEY CAN KEEP UP WITH YOU AND YOUR CAREER.

Once you get a job, send a thank-you note and periodic updates to your references. They'll appreciate it and may recommend or refer you to others as you advance in your career.

To Do:

List three people who would make good references for you.

1. _____

2. _____

3. _____

Describe why these people would make good references.

_____

_____

_____

_____

_____

_____

Volunteering

A volunteer or community service position is just like a job. As a volunteer, however, you don't get paid. The managers will depend on you to perform a job and will give their time for your training and supervision. A volunteer position is the same as a paid position in terms of your responsibilities to the organization.

You may want a volunteer position because of community service requirements from school. Or you may want it on your resume because it will help you in the future with college and paid positions. So you should apply for the position professionally with a resume.

Distributing at College Fairs

The admissions representatives are waiting to meet you. You can hand your resume to college recruiters, smile, and speak a few words about yourself. The lasting impression, however, will be made by the resume you have written about your high school years. Colleges put that resume into their records. This may even get you calls from college recruiters if they are interested.

Applying for Summer Programs

You may have to complete an application and personal statement for summer programs. In addition to those documents, you could enclose a resume. This one-page document serves as a quick review for the admissions committee for the summer program. Some programs can be very competitive, and a resume could set you apart from other applicants. You would look professional, sincere, and ready to go.

Networking with Friends of Parents, Neighbors, Former Teachers, and Coaches

Networking, which means introducing yourself and your goals to *everyone,* is one of the most successful methods of the job search. Someone in your network may know of a job, internship, or educational program that would be perfect for you. If you tell people about your interests, they will keep you in mind.

One day you might get a call along these lines: "I found out about this internship, and I thought of you. Would you be interested?" Your future could be changed because of a lead like this.

You might think that people you know will be aware of all you have done in high school. In reality, they may be vaguely familiar with your athletic achievements or recall that you did really well in science. But they won't know everything you have done in and outside of school.

> **What's the Difference Between a Mentor and a Network?**
>
> What's the difference between a person who is your mentor and a person who is in your network? A mentor is your regular career and educational advisor. This person can make recommendations for courses and internships that will help you with your career. A member of your network is an occasional contact regarding job leads or referrals.

The best way to network is to keep in touch with people, keep your resume up-to-date, and give it to people. You cannot be bashful when you're trying to develop a career and want to succeed.

Informational Interviewing

Informational interviewing is a common practice among job seekers, college graduates, and individuals interested in a specific career. The goal is to find a person within a career field, or even a company in which you may like to work, and ask for an appointment to discuss the individual's job. You might hand or mail the person your resume with a cover letter asking for an informational interview. Most professionals know what an informational interview is. Don't be bashful about asking for 10 or 15 minutes. All the individual can do is say no, and you'll move on to someone who has more time.

Do some research before the interview about the company. Check its Web site. Ask for its annual report (a booklet published by every public company available for free). Ask a receptionist for a brochure on the company.

Write down a few questions, but don't be afraid to ask spontaneous ones. Sometimes they are the best and will get you the most information. Examples of questions are, "Do you really like your job?" and "What do you enjoy most and least about your work?"

How do you find the name of someone to interview? You might read about a person in a newspaper article; hear the person's name on a talk show; read a name on the Web; or be referred by someone in your network.

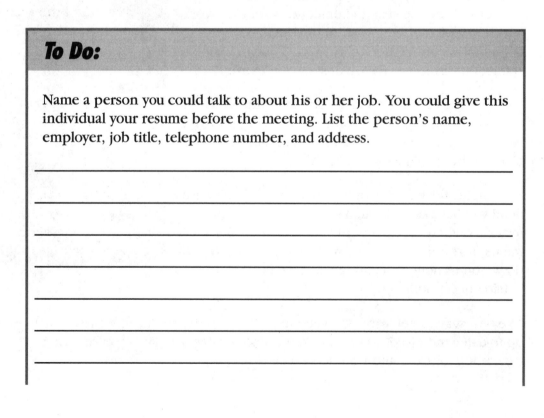

To Do:

Name a person you could talk to about his or her job. You could give this individual your resume before the meeting. List the person's name, employer, job title, telephone number, and address.

_____

_____

_____

_____

_____

_____

List three questions you could ask in an informational interview.

1. _____

   _____

   _____

   _____

2. _____

   _____

   _____

   _____

3. _____

   _____

   _____

   _____

Joining College Activities

It's possible that when you begin attending college, you will want to be selected for a publication's editorial board or some other prestigious group or activity. The student leadership may want to see what you have done in high school before offering you a position. A good resume will make an impression and land you the opportunity to be part of a competitive college organization.

Using Your Resume

As you learned in this chapter, you can use a resume in many ways—not just in a job search. As you go on to the rest of the book, keep these many ways in mind. They will help you write a great, focused resume!

To Do:

Make a list of potential ways you can use a resume within the next year. This list will give you a purpose for working on your resume and keeping it up-to-date.

_____

_____

_____

_____

_____

_____

_____

_____

_____

_____

_____

_____

_____

_____

_____

_____

_____

_____

_____

_____

Understanding Resume Types

"I see your most recent work experience was lawn mowing."

hree standard resume types are used. This chapter introduces you to these types and emphasizes the ones most useful to high school students.

The three major resume types are as follows:

- ✉ **Chronological.** Describes employment and education, starting with the current or most recent event and ending with the least recent.

- ✉ **Functional.** Organizes your background by areas of skill and experience, such as computers, customer service, writing, and languages.

- ✉ **Combination (also called a targeted resume).** Includes both of the above sections. A summary of skills appears at the top, followed by employment and education. A combination resume is also called a targeted resume because it presents all relevant information in a way that appeals to your target.

Resume Types Most Useful to Students

High school students usually use two of these resume types: a chronological resume for college applications and a targeted resume for jobs and internships. As a student, you do not want to write a functional resume at this time in your life because it requires extensive experience in many areas.

Chronological Resume for College Applications

A chronological college resume is a comprehensive resume not targeted in a specific direction, as it would be if you were pursuing a particular career. It is a complete presentation of your qualifications. It lists many items, including the following: important academic courses and workshops; good grades; sports and other activities; honors and awards; work-study programs and internships; service learning; and employment.

Targeted Resume for Jobs and Internships

A targeted resume highlights the skills and experiences that you want to promote to a potential employer or other individual.

Whether you realize it, you do have skills that can be highlighted. These skills are developed in many ways, including the following: educational courses; work experiences; internships; volunteer activities; extracurricular activities; reading; interests and hobbies; sports; travel; interpersonal relationships; and study attitudes and habits.

To Do:

Name three things that you are involved in that will reflect well on your resume and will help you develop new skills.

1. _____

2. _____

3. _____

Name three things that you could get involved in that will help you develop new skills.

1. _____

2. _____

3. _____

The rest of this chapter discusses guidelines for the two resume formats most often used by students and shows examples of each.

College Resume: For College Applications, Scholarships, Mentors, and College Fairs

Your college application, personal statement, and resume will be your introduction to the admissions committee. If you would like to attend a particular college for four years, make your application package stand out. If you have a major in mind, make sure that your resume includes all your experience, honors, and activities in that area. You also will use your college resume to apply for scholarships, to hand out at college fairs, and to find a mentor.

Keep in mind these college resume pointers:

✉ A college resume is your complete academic and experience profile.

✉ It is not targeted toward any field.

✉ The reader obtains a broad review of your education, experience, activities, honors, and other background information.

✉ You may or may not include an objective or skills statement in this type of resume.

Emily's College Resume Example

Emily used the following resume, along with her application and personal statement, to apply to colleges. During this time, she emphasized her writing, teaching, and theater background. Her major was declared as creative writing.

As you will see in later examples in this chapter, Emily changed her mind about future goals after holding two internships.

> **TIP** EMILY'S RESUME EXAMPLES ARE HERE TO GET YOU THINKING ABOUT YOUR OWN BACKGROUND AND SHOW HOW MUCH YOU CAN DO TO AFFECT YOUR FUTURE NOW. DON'T BE DISCOURAGED IF YOUR LIST OF ACTIVITIES IS SHORTER THAN HERS. YOUR EXPERIENCES, NO MATTER HOW FEW OR HOW MANY, CAN BE USED TO CREATE A UNIQUE, GREAT-LOOKING RESUME, TOO.

CASE STUDY

EMILY THOMPSON
43 Village Court, Westboro, MD 00000
Home: (000) 555-5555
E-mail: thompson@ari.net

EDUCATION

Westboro High School, Westboro, MD. Expect to graduate May 1998.
Academic Honors:
Honor Roll, average GPA 3.8/4.0, 1994-present
Advanced Placement: U.S. History and English coursework
Activities:
Editor-in-Chief, *Phoenix* Literary Arts Magazine, 1996-1998
Co-teacher, Creative Writing, Westboro High School, Spring 1998
Co-teacher, Introductory Theater Arts, Westboro High School, Spring 1998
Maryland State Forensics League, President
 Debate National Competitor, Kansas City, KS (1998), Milwaukee, WI (1997), Detroit,
  MI (1996)
 2nd Place, Regional Competition, 1996
 Mock Trial Competition, individually recognized for outstanding performance, 1996
Dramatic Theater: *Twelve Angry Jurors; Flowers for Algernon*; leading role in *You Can't
Take It with You*

> Student teaching experience

> Creative writing interests are everywhere

WORKSHOPS

Hawaiian Language and Culture, Maui Community College, Maui, HI, Fall 1997
Writing and Thinking, Lewis College, Seattle, WA, Summer 1997
National Outdoor Leadership School, Lander, WY, Summer 1997
Andre Braugher ("Homicide" series) Shakespeare Workshop, Winter 1996
Writer's Workshop, State University, Frederick, MD, Summer 1996

> Theater and public speaking experience

HONORS AND RECOGNITION

Recognized by County Public Schools for community contribution, 1997
Winner of Redmond College's "Women Writing about Women" Competition,
 April 1997, one of three selected out of 140 portfolios entered

PUBLISHED POETRY

Salt of the Earth Literary Magazine
Singing Sands Review
The Apprentice Writer
Featured reader in publicized Fells Point and Baltimore poetry readings

EXPERIENCE

Internship, Haleakala National Park, Maui, HI   Sept.-Dec. 1997
 Interpretation and special projects.
Legal Assistant, Trafalgar & Associates, Ft. Collins, CO   Summer 1996
 Legal research, office administration, and assistant to attorney in litigation.
Teacher's Aide, Newton Elementary School, Baltimore, MD   Spring 1995

COMPUTER SKILLS

PC and Macintosh: Windows 95, Microsoft Office Suite, Word 7.0, WordPerfect 6.1,
 Internet

More College Resume Examples

Kathlene Y. McNamee, a professional resume writer in Butte, Montana, helped a local high school student create the following resume. The student wanted to find a job that would help her save money for college and gain practical experience. The chronological college resume format worked for this student, because her objectives were not targeted to a specific field or employer.

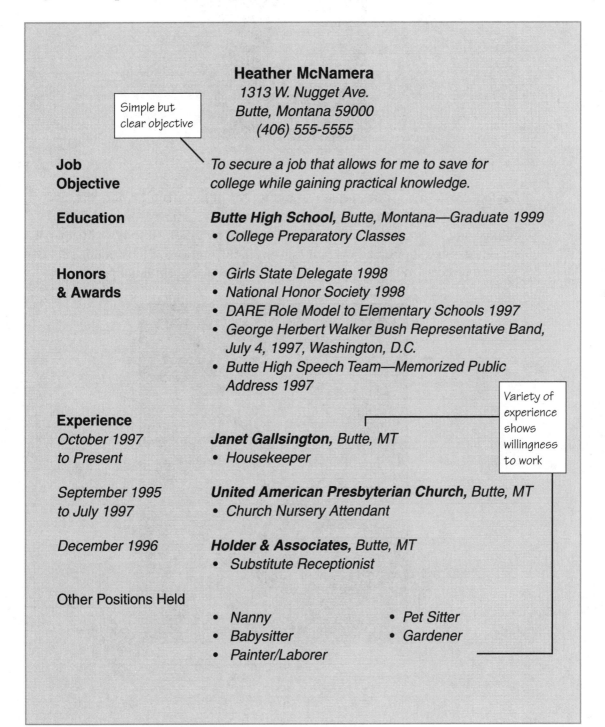

Heather McNamera

1313 W. Nugget Ave.
Butte, Montana 59000
(406) 555-5555

Simple but clear objective

Job Objective

To secure a job that allows for me to save for college while gaining practical knowledge.

Education

Butte High School, *Butte, Montana—Graduate 1999*
- *College Preparatory Classes*

Honors & Awards

- *Girls State Delegate 1998*
- *National Honor Society 1998*
- *DARE Role Model to Elementary Schools 1997*
- *George Herbert Walker Bush Representative Band, July 4, 1997, Washington, D.C.*
- *Butte High Speech Team—Memorized Public Address 1997*

Experience

October 1997 to Present

Janet Gallsington, *Butte, MT*
- *Housekeeper*

Variety of experience shows willingness to work

September 1995 to July 1997

United American Presbyterian Church, *Butte, MT*
- *Church Nursery Attendant*

December 1996

Holder & Associates, *Butte, MT*
- *Substitute Receptionist*

Other Positions Held

- *Nanny*
- *Babysitter*
- *Painter/Laborer*
- *Pet Sitter*
- *Gardener*

Heather McNamera

Gayle Bernstein, a professional resume writer in Indianapolis, Indiana, assisted the following student who had two goals with his resume: to attend college and to become a college baseball team member. Note how dual Goal statements are supported by dual Achievement sections. The student sent the resume directly to college coaches and received four scholarship offers.

Terry Lantz

Terry Lantz
Vandalia High School
16000 Berry Street • Indianapolis, Indiana 00000 • (317) 000-0000

ACADEMIC GOAL

To attend a college or university focusing on Business, Engineering, Math, or Science. Long-term goal is to attain a graduate degree in my chosen field.

ATHLETIC GOAL

To utilize my experience and strong background of 12 years to become a member of a college/university baseball team.

ACADEMIC ACHIEVEMENTS/ACTIVITIES

> Academic Achievements back up first goal

Vandalia High School, Indianapolis, Indiana
G. P. A.: 3.68   CLASS RANK: 59/727
National Honor Society
Key Club Member

ATHLETIC ACHIEVEMENTS

JUNIOR YEAR, 1997-1998
• **Varsity Baseball** (Marion County Championship Team; Semi-State Finalists)
  * Left Field (Lead-Off Hitter)
  * Second Team All County
• **Varsity Soccer** (State Runner-Up 1997; State Champions, 1998)
  * Defense
  * Academic All-State

> Athletic Achievements back up second goal

SOPHOMORE YEAR, 1996-1997
• **Reserve Baseball**
  * Left Field
  * Indiana Amateur Baseball Association All-Star Selection
• **Reserve Soccer**
  * Defense

FRESHMAN YEAR, 1995-1996
• **Baseball**
  * Left Field
  * Indiana Amateur Baseball Association All-Star Selection
• **Reserve Soccer**
  * Defense
• **Wrestling**
  * Record — 19/3

VARSITY STATISTICS/Junior Year/1998 Season

Team Leader

	Avg.	Sig.	OB%	G	AB	Run	H	1B	2B	3B	HR
Spring	.289	.451	.513	30*	85	25*	24	14	6*	3*	1
Summer	.379	.539	.602	16	49	17*	18	11	5*	1	0
	RBI	**TB**	**SC**	**OE**	**HP**	**BB**	**SO**	**SB**	**SA**	**SB%**	
Spring	15	40	4	7	4	31*	20	7*	9*	.779	
Summer	8	26	2	3	0	17*	8	8*	10*	.817*	

Targeted Resume: For Jobs, Internships, and Service Learning

A targeted resume is directed toward a specific position or career goal. The skills that are highlighted are carefully selected to interest the reader. Remember these facts about targeted resumes:

- ✉ The targeted resume summarizes your skills and uses *key words* relevant to the target position. Key words reflect the skills needed for a job. For instance, if you're applying for an office clerk position, the critical key words would be *computer skills, verbal skills, customer service, report writing, proofreading, editing, teamwork,* and *organization.*

- ✉ A targeted resume may not include all of your experiences if they are not relevant to the position. For instance, suppose you're applying for a data-entry position. The manager does not need to know all your course names, that your soccer team ranked third, or that you worked at the freshman donut sale.

- ✉ The targeted resume should be one page. As you gain more skills, you may need to delete older and less relevant material.

CASE STUDY

Emily's Targeted Resume Examples

Emily wrote the following targeted resumes for different objectives at different times in high school:

- ✉ **Example 1.** Applying for an internship with a nonprofit association or legislative office.

- ✉ **Example 2.** Applying for a volunteer interpreter position with the Department of the Interior, Haleakala National Park, Hawaii.

- ✉ **Example 3.** Applying for a trail worker position with Volunteer-in-Parks, Kings Canyon, California.

Each resume required different information. The resumes became shorter and shorter because the resume for trail worker did not require the academic details of the first resume.

Targeted Resume: Example 1

While a junior, Emily used the following resume to apply for a summer internship or page position in Congress. She highlighted skills described in the internship ads. She was interested in writing, research, and gaining experience toward a career as an educator or lawyer.

Key words

Highlights of writing and research experience

EMILY THOMPSON
43 Village Court, Westboro, MD 00000
Home: (000) 555-5555
E-mail: thompson@ari.net

OBJECTIVE: Internship with a nonprofit association or legislative office

SUMMARY OF RELEVANT SKILLS AND EXPERIENCE

Writing and Research Experience

Skilled researcher of political and policy issues with debate league. Course emphasis has been on English and writing. Editor of the *Phoenix* literary/art publication. Published poetry in school, community, and college literary publications. Attended two college writing workshops for critical thinking and writing.

Communications Skills

Four years in theater with the lead in a popular comedy. Selected for highly competitive Shakespeare workshop. National competitor in debate competitions. Invited to read poetry at public venues with students and established poets.

Computer Skills

Experience with PCs and Macintosh; Windows 95, Microsoft Office, Word 7.0, WordPerfect 6.1, Internet; keyboard over 45 wpm.

EDUCATION

Westboro High School, Westboro, MD. Expect to graduate May 1998.

Computer skills are always important

Academic Honors:
Honor Roll, average GPA 3.8/4.0, 1994-present
Advanced Placement U.S. History and English coursework

Activities:
Maryland State Forensics League, President
    Debate National Competitor, Milwaukee,WI (1997), Detroit, MI (1996)
    2nd Place, Regional Competition, 1996
    Mock Trial Competition, individually recognized for outstanding performance, 1996
Editor-in-Chief, *Phoenix* Literary Art Magazine, 1996-present
Twelve Angry Jurors; Flowers for Algernon; leading role in *You Can't Take It with You*

WORKSHOPS

Andre Braugher ("Homicide") Shakespeare Workshop, Winter 1996
Writer's Workshop, State University, Frederick, MD, Summer 1996

HONORS AND RECOGNITION

Recognized by County Public Schools for community contribution, Spring 1997
Winner of Redmond College's "Women Writing about Women" Competition, April 1997
Honorable Mention, County Public Schools Poetry Competition, 1996

PUBLISHED WORKS

Salt of the Earth Literary Magazine, *Singing Sands Review, The Apprentice Writer*. Featured reader in publicized Fells Point and Baltimore poetry readings.

EXPERIENCE

Legal Assistant, Trafalgar & Associates, Ft. Collins, CO, Summer 1996
    Legal research, office administration, and assistant to attorney who specialized in litigation.

Congress lost its page budget that year. So Emily attended a creative writing workshop and completed the National Outdoor Leadership School. This was the beginning of her interest in environmental science and writing.

When her original plan didn't work out, Emily Thompson participated in outdoor leadership training in Wyoming between her junior and senior years. This experience turned her career ideas in a new direction.

Targeted Resume: Example 2

After such a great summer, Emily wanted a senior year fall internship. She applied to Haleakala National Park in Hawaii for a volunteer interpreter position. As an interpreter, she would have to research a topic (for example, plants and wildlife) and give 20-minute presentations to tourists.

This targeted resume emphasized her communication skills and outdoor training. All of her honors, awards, and workshops were not relevant. Here is the resume she used to apply to the Department of the Interior. Emily got the internship!

> **TIP** NOTICE HOW EMILY'S OUTDOOR LEADERSHIP TRAINING IS LISTED AT THE TOP OF HER SKILLS SUMMARY. THIS TRAINING WAS IMPORTANT IN TARGETING THE NATIONAL PARK SERVICE INTERNSHIP. AS YOU CREATE YOUR OWN RESUME, WATCH FOR WAYS TO EMPHASIZE EXPERIENCE MOST RELEVANT TO THE JOB.

Skills in leadership, research, and public speaking are highlighted

EMILY THOMPSON
43 Village Court, Westboro, MD 00000
Home: (000) 555-5555
E-mail: thompson@ari.net

OBJECTIVE: Volunteer Interpreter, Department of the Interior, Haleakala National Park, Maui, HI

Outdoor Leadership School listed at the top

SUMMARY OF RELEVANT SKILLS AND EXPERIENCE

Outdoor Leadership Training
National Outdoor Leadership School, Lander, Wyoming, Summer 1997. Graduated Rocky Mountain Horsepacking course, involving one week of ranch experience and two weeks of backcountry travel in the Wind River range. Trained in minimum impact camping, backpacking, and horsepacking. Emphasis on backcountry leadership skills necessary to lead future personal expeditions: safety and judgment, leadership and teamwork, outdoor skills, environmental ethics, and horse handling and packing skills.

Writing and Research Experience
Skilled researcher and debater. Course emphasis has been on English and writing. Editor of the *Phoenix* literary publication.

Communications Skills
Four years in theater with the lead in a popular comedy. Selected for highly competitive Shakespeare workshop. National competitor in debate competitions. Invited to read poetry at public readings with students and established poets.

EDUCATION

Activities, Workshops, and Honors are streamlined and targeted

Westboro High School, Westboro, MD. Expect to graduate May 1998.
Academic Honors:
Honor Roll, average GPA 3.8/4.0, 1994-present
Activities:
Maryland State Forensics League, President 2nd Place, Regional Competition, 1996
Editor-in-Chief, *Phoenix* Literary Art Magazine, 1996-present

PUBLISHED WORKS

Salt of the Earth Literary Magazine, *Singing Sands Review, The Apprentice Writer.* Featured reader in publicized Fells Point and Baltimore poetry readings.

EXPERIENCE

Legal Assistant, Trafalgar & Associates, Ft. Collins, CO   Summer 1996

In the fall of her senior year, Emily gained great experience as a volunteer interpreter at a National Park in Hawaii.

Targeted Resume: Example 3

For the summer after graduation, Emily used the next resume to apply for an internship at Kings Canyon, California, as a trail worker in the Volunteer-in-Parks Program. She wanted to gain environmental experience that involved hard labor.

This application did not require specific information on honors, activities, workshops, and publications. Emily needed to show that she could backpack, cut through rocks to make switchbacks, and live in a tent for two months. She succeeded as a trail worker.

Her interests in the environment have evolved. She hopes for a self-designed major in environmental science and creative writing.

> **TIP** NOTICE THAT THE NEXT RESUME HAS NEW KEY WORDS, WHICH REFLECT THE SKILLS NEEDED FOR THE TRAIL WORKER INTERNSHIP THAT EMILY WANTED.

Key words

EMILY THOMPSON
43 Village Court
Westboro, MD 00000
Home: (000) 555-5555
E-mail: thompson@ari.net

OBJECTIVE: Trail Worker, Volunteer-in-Parks, Kings Canyon, California

SUMMARY OF RELEVANT SKILLS AND EXPERIENCE

Outdoor Leadership Experience

National Outdoor Leadership School, Lander, WY, Summer 1997
Graduated Rocky Mountain Horsepacking course involving one week of ranch experience
and two weeks of backcountry travel in the Wind River range. Trained in minimum impact
camping, backpacking, and horsepacking. Emphasis on backcountry leadership skills
necessary to lead future personal expeditions: safety and judgment, leadership and teamwork,
outdoor skills, environmental ethics, and horse handling and packing skills.

Outdoor experience

Interpretation Skills

Internship, Haleakala National Park, Maui, HI, Fall 1997
Interpretation at high-volume visitor center and development of special projects, including
park displays and 20-minute naturalist visitor programs. Hiked inside the volcano six miles.

High School Public Speaking
Experienced researcher and writer in high school and community publications. Four years'
experience in theater and debate competitions.

Field hockey is now mentioned

Sports and Athletic Experience

Member, varsity field hockey team, 1996
Enjoy hiking, backpacking, and camping
Physically fit

Fitness is important in the backcountry

EDUCATION

Westboro High School, Westboro, MD. Graduated May 1998.
Honor Roll, average GPA 3.8/4.0, 1994-1998

All awards and workshops are deleted

EXPERIENCE

Legal Assistant, Trafalgar & Associates, Ft. Collins, CO   Summer 1996

More Targeted Resume Examples

If you think that you're too young for a resume, look at the next two targeted resumes. Both were created by professional resume writer Gayle Bernstein of Indianapolis, Indiana, for student Karen Jones.

When Karen was in sixth grade, she used the first resume to apply for a volunteer position with her school library (and got the job). By highlighting her skills at the top and then listing her work experience in family businesses, Karen showed great ambition and ability at a young age.

Now a high school freshman, Karen distributed the second resume at a local job fair. Although too young for a paying job, Karen was invited to the fair because local employers desperately needed help and wanted to line up teen workers in advance.

Karen Jones

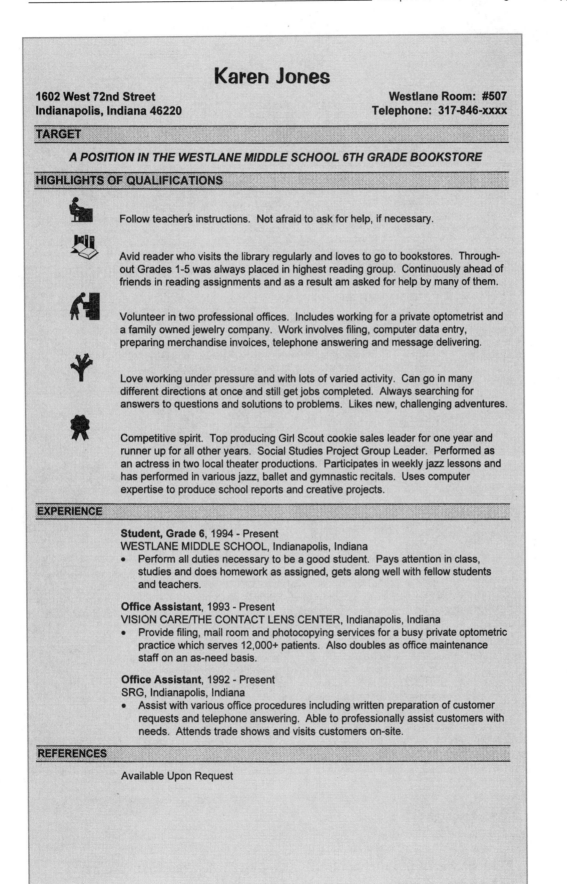

Karen Jones

1602 West 72nd Street
Indianapolis, Indiana 46220

Westlane Room: #507
Telephone: 317-846-xxxx

TARGET

A POSITION IN THE WESTLANE MIDDLE SCHOOL 6TH GRADE BOOKSTORE

HIGHLIGHTS OF QUALIFICATIONS

Follow teacher's instructions. Not afraid to ask for help, if necessary.

Avid reader who visits the library regularly and loves to go to bookstores. Throughout Grades 1-5 was always placed in highest reading group. Continuously ahead of friends in reading assignments and as a result am asked for help by many of them.

Volunteer in two professional offices. Includes working for a private optometrist and a family owned jewelry company. Work involves filing, computer data entry, preparing merchandise invoices, telephone answering and message delivering.

Love working under pressure and with lots of varied activity. Can go in many different directions at once and still get jobs completed. Always searching for answers to questions and solutions to problems. Likes new, challenging adventures.

Competitive spirit. Top producing Girl Scout cookie sales leader for one year and runner up for all other years. Social Studies Project Group Leader. Performed as an actress in two local theater productions. Participates in weekly jazz lessons and has performed in various jazz, ballet and gymnastic recitals. Uses computer expertise to produce school reports and creative projects.

EXPERIENCE

Student, Grade 6, 1994 - Present
WESTLANE MIDDLE SCHOOL, Indianapolis, Indiana
- Perform all duties necessary to be a good student. Pays attention in class, studies and does homework as assigned, gets along well with fellow students and teachers.

Office Assistant, 1993 - Present
VISION CARE/THE CONTACT LENS CENTER, Indianapolis, Indiana
- Provide filing, mail room and photocopying services for a busy private optometric practice which serves 12,000+ patients. Also doubles as office maintenance staff on an as-need basis.

Office Assistant, 1992 - Present
SRG, Indianapolis, Indiana
- Assist with various office procedures including written preparation of customer requests and telephone answering. Able to professionally assist customers with needs. Attends trade shows and visits customers on-site.

REFERENCES

Available Upon Request

Karen Jones

1602 West 72nd Street ▪ Indianapolis, Indiana 46220 ▪ 317-259-xxxx

JOB TARGET / HIGHLIGHTS OF QUALIFICATIONS

A part-time **Retail Sales** position that will use my already proven **customer service, administrative,** and **organizational** abilities.

- Able to effectively follow instructions while quickly adapting to existing operations.
- Assisted with office procedures in multiple professional environments. Computer literate.
- Maintains accurate and detailed records, merchandise invoices, and product inventories.
- Enjoys working under pressure and with lots of varied activity while completing jobs.
- Competitive spirit. Top producing fund-raiser, special project group member, community service leader, and theater performer.

EDUCATION

NORTH CENTRAL HIGH SCHOOL, Indianapolis, Indiana
College Preparatory Program with goal toward college / Class of 2001   GPA: 3.0 / 4.0
Activity: Varsity and Junior Girls Basketball Manager, 1997 - 1998

PROFESSIONAL AND VOLUNTEER EXPERIENCE

Grade 5 Sunday School Teacher's Aide, 9/97 - Present
BETH-EL ZEDECK, Indianapolis, Indiana
- Assist classroom teacher with 18 students. Includes recording attendance, collecting and documenting $20-25 in weekly charity donations, implementing tests, making and assembling photocopies, and monitoring class during teacher's absence.

Babysitter, 9/97 - Present
BETH-EL ZEDECK, Indianapolis, Indiana
- Selected by congregational leader to provide child care services for infants to 6 year olds on an as-needed basis.

Bookstore Staff Member, 1996 - 1997
WESTLANE MIDDLE SCHOOL, Indianapolis, Indiana
- Elected by fellow students to handle multiple responsibilities in on-site bookstore three days per week. Opened and closed facility. Sold books and miscellaneous supplies. Completed inventory reports.

Office Assistant, 1993 - 1995
VISION CARE, PC, Indianapolis, Indiana
- Provided filing, mail room, and photocopying services for a busy private optometry practice which served 12,000+ patients. Doubled as office maintenance staff on an as-need basis.

Office Assistant, 1992 - Present
SRG, Indianapolis, Indiana
- Assist with varied office procedures including written preparation of customer requests. Professionally respond to telephone calls for individual orders from customers located throughout the nation. Participate in out-of-town customer sales trips; attend trade shows.

EXTRACURRICULAR ACTIVITIES

Beth-El Zedeck United Synagogue Youth (USY), 9/97 - Present
- Work independently and as a team member while participating in varied service projects. Managed booth at annual fundraising event that contributed to earning $3,500-$4,000 for year-round activities. Scheduled to attend regional convention in Cleveland, Ohio. Attended regional convention in Detroit, Michigan (Summer of 1997).

Beth-El Teens, 1995 - 1997 / Secretary, 1996
- Actively participated in youth group with 60 members.

Camp Broadway / Jewish Community Center, Summer 1996, 1997
- Held lead and minor roles in local "sold to capacity" theater productions. Assisted with set design, attaining costumes, and selling tickets.

To Do:

Which type of resume would you like to write as your first resume: college or targeted? _____

Resume- Writing Exercises

3

"I've never had a job! What could I possibly put on a resume?"

Many students think that they don't have anything to include on a resume. Does that describe you? If so, think again. This chapter will guide you through the various sections of your resume except the Skills section. You will write the Skills section of your resume in the next chapter. If you answer all the questions that follow, your resume will be well underway.

Take a Section-by-Section Approach

A section-by-section approach is the best way to write your resume. By focusing on each section separately, you will think about every aspect of your high school education and experience. You will list information under each section's heading, which emphasizes its importance.

By listing information in resume sections, you (and those reading your resume) will recognize the significance of everything you've done. Don't worry if you have little or nothing to write for certain sections. Include whatever information you can now. Then get busy. Find activities and courses that appeal to you and are worth adding to your resume. You can do the following:

- ✉ Join a group or club that interests you.

- ✉ Take a course or workshop in a specialized field.

- ✉ Pursue relevant work experience.

- ✉ Apply for an internship.

- ✉ Do volunteer work.

- ✉ Apply for a responsible service-learning program.

> **TIP** TALK TO YOUR TEACHERS, COUNSELORS, AND SCHOOL LIBRARIAN ABOUT WORKSHOPS, ACTIVITIES, AND OTHER OPPORTUNITIES AND WHERE TO FIND THEM.

This chapter now gets down to the business of resume writing. You will begin to develop your resume piece-by-piece into a comprehensive document that represents *you*. At this point it doesn't matter which resume type you write—a chronological college resume or a targeted resume. You simply need to write down the basic information.

CASE STUDY

List Everything Now—Fine-Tune It Later

As you can see from Emily's examples in Chapter 2, she selected the information that was relevant to the particular job she was trying to get. This was much easier once she had a comprehensive list of everything she'd done. For example, field hockey appeared on her original activities list but only on one resume. Her debate experience appeared on each resume, but in a way that fit its purpose.

Your resume's target will dictate how to present your background. For now, write down all the information you might use in your resume.

Contact Information

The prospective employer needs to see your name in large bold type with your address, telephone number, and e-mail address clearly listed. Get creative and arrange this section any way you choose. See Chapter 5 for more formatting ideas.

Here are some examples of how to arrange this information. Put a check mark next to the formats you like.

SAMANTHA A. GREENE

17 Cherokee Avenue / Catonsville, MD 20233
(555) 555-0000 / E-mail: greene@net.net

KIERA M. KRUEGER
79 Carmel Street
Long Beach, California 95900
(555) 555-9999

CAROLYN ANNE HOBART

One Valley Lane, Utica, New York 76655
Home (555) 555-7777
E-mail: hobart@com.com

CHRIS LANSING

53 Ridge Road, Katy, Texas 99999   Home (555) 555-6666
E-Mail: lansing@net.net

Michael G. Anders

500 Delaware Street / Pemberton, WA 95544 / (555) 555-4444

RHONDA S. ROBERTS
43 KING BLVD.
DETROIT, MI 88888
(555) 555-2222

THOMAS BAKER, III
47 Creek Place
Chevy Chase, MD 45554

Phone/fax: (555) 555-8888   E-mail: baker@net.net

STEVEN APPLEGATE

42C W. 90th Avenue   Phone (555) 555-4321
New York, NY 77777   Beeper (555) 555-1234

Nancy E. Day

School Address   *Home Address*
14 Smythe Street   121 Long Street
Ft. Washington, MD 55555   Westminster, MD 55555
(555) 555-0000–Messages   (555)555-5555–Home

TIP THE ARRANGEMENT OF YOUR CONTACT INFORMATION MIGHT DEPEND ON HOW CROWDED YOUR RESUME IS. (YES, YOUR RESUME MAY GET CROWDED!) NOTE HOW YOU CAN PUT YOUR ADDRESS AND PHONE NUMBER ON ONE LINE TO SAVE SPACE.

To Do:

Write your name and contact information in an arrangement that you can follow when you go to your computer to lay out your resume. You may want to try several arrangements, based on the examples.

_____

_____

_____

_____

Education and Academics

The basic setup for your Education section includes the name, city, and state of your high school and your expected graduation date. Then list specific academic information, such as GPA, college entrance test scores, and special courses. Your GPA can be listed if it is over 3.0. Include courses in languages, advanced placement, computers, and electives.

Catonsville High School, Catonsville, MD
Graduation expected June 1999
Gifted and Talented English and Social Studies courses, 1997-present
Advanced Placement U.S. History, 1998

THOMAS R. PROCTOR HIGH SCHOOL, Utica, NY
Graduation June 1999
Overall GPA 3.0/4.0
Computer courses: PCs with Windows, Microsoft Word, and Microsoft Excel

CARIZZO SPRINGS HIGH SCHOOL, Carizzo Springs, TX. Expect to graduate May 1999.
Special course work:
Agriculture and Livestock Management
Biology I, II and Environmental Sciences I
Spanish I, II, III
Business Management and PCs

California High School, San Ramon, CA. Graduated May 1998.
Grade Point Average 3.62
SAT Verbal 560; Math 710
Advanced Placement:
AP Calculus
AP English Composition and Literature

To Do:

What is your high school's name, city, and state?

_____

_____

What year are you expected to graduate? _____

What special courses have you taken or are you taking? Include the grades you received if meaningful.

_____

_____

_____

_____

_____

List your SAT and ACT test scores if they would make a good impression.

_____

_____

List your GPA if it is above 3.0. _____

Honors and Awards

Your honors will demonstrate your dedication and skill level. Here are some examples of the Honors section of high school resumes:

HONORS

National Honor Society	1997-present
National Merit Scholar Honorable Mention	1998
Second Place in Catonsville High School Math Contest	1998

Musical Honors
- Distinguished Maryland Scholar, Talent in the Arts finalist
- Passed Associated Board of the Royal School of Music theory tests with distinction grades 2 and 5
- Passed Associated Board of the Royal School of Music practical exams with distinction grades 4 and 5

ATHLETIC AWARDS

Varsity Basketball, MVP	1998
Athlete of the Year, County School System	1997
All-Baltimore County, Honorable Mention (basketball)	1997

HONORS

Region 81 Champion Team Roper, 1998

Rodeo State Finalist (Calf Roping and Team Roping), 1997, 1998

Lone Star Farmer, 1997

Member, 4-H Club—raised show lambs

Honors
- Honored by Bloomsburg Parks & Recreation Association for outstanding service for volunteerism for early childhood after-school program, 1997-1998
- Received third place, Candid Photography Contest, *Washington Post,* May 1997
- Received a certificate for participation in children's programs, Bethany Baptist Church, 1997

To Do:

List your honors and awards next, including dates. For example, if you were a champion swimmer or received a certificate for participating in an essay contest, write that information here. You never know when you might need the item for a targeted resume. You can organize and edit the honors list as needed when you write a resume for a certain purpose.

List honors you received through community events and teams.

_____

_____

List honors you received through your studies.

_____

_____

_____

_____

List honors you received through special academic programs.

_____

_____

_____

_____

List honors you received through contests.

_____

_____

_____

_____

List honors you received through your school extracurricular activities and sports.

_____

_____

_____

_____

Activities

Activities can give you valuable exposure to future careers. For example, participating in the photography club could lead to a photojournalism career. If you enjoy the debate club, you may want to investigate a legal career. Taking part in a tree-planting day may inspire you to consider a gardening or environmental career. These activities may give you an advantage when applying for jobs in your field of interest.

Through your high school activities, employers and college admissions recruiters will determine your characteristics and skills. For example, these activities indicate certain qualities:

- ⊠ **Sports.** Leadership, competitive, team player, meets schedules, performs under pressure, cooperates with others, manages schoolwork, and practices.

- ⊠ **Theater and public speaking.** Communications skills, ability to work with the public, articulate, persuasive, outgoing, teamwork, competitive, organized.

- ⊠ **Journalism/yearbook/poetry.** Writing, research, editing, interviewing skills, meets deadlines, interpersonal skills, organized, teamwork, computer and publishing knowledge.

On your resume, you do not need to use the words *debate, theater*, and *journalism* next to the activity. The words are shown here to give you ideas of school activities. You would use the heading "Activities" above this section on your resume.

Debate

Alta Vista Debate League
- Active Competitor, Duo and Oral Interpretation, 1997-present
- Moot Court, 1996-present

Theater

Riverside Community Theater: *The Miracle Worker,* 1998; *West Side Story,* 1997; *Under the Moonlight,* 1996

Journalism

The Patriot, Washington High School monthly newspaper
 Reporter, 1997-present
 — Conduct interviews
 — Write news and feature stories
 — Assist with layout and proofreading

Writing	Two poems published in *Ellipsis,* Key High School's literary magazine Poem published in the *National Anthology of Young American Writers*	

Art	— Several pieces of visual art shown at Williamsburg High School's Showcase, 1997 — Pencil drawing hung in the County Board of Education Building, 1996	

Sports	Varsity Field Hockey Team—second in league	1998
	St. William of York Church Softball	1998
	Portland Parks Softball and Basketball	1995-1998

Music	All-County and All-State Trumpet	1997-1998
	Steel Drum Band, Pep Band, Jazz Band	1996-1998
	Towsen State University Honor Band	1997

To Do:

Record all your activities in high school. Include the group or organization names, the titles of any positions you held, and your participation dates. Make a complete list here that you can edit later. Add to the list as you participate in new activities.

_____

_____

_____

_____

_____

_____

_____

_____

_____

_____

Honors and Activities (Combined Section)

If you have a short list of honors and activities, consider combining this information into one section. For instance, if you have two honors and two activities, then a combined section would be best. Here are examples of formats to use.

HONORS AND ACTIVITIES

Medical Explorer, 1997-present
Manager, Varsity Boys' Soccer Team, 1997
Students Against Drunk Driving, 1996, 1997
International Thespian Society, inducted 1996

Honors and Activities

Student Government Association
    Senior Class Treasurer, 1997-present
    Active member, 1995-present
All-County and All-State Trumpet, 1996-1997
Pit Orchestra, member, 1995-present

ACTIVITIES AND HONOR SOCIETIES

National Honor Society	1996-1998
National Art Honor Society Member	1995-1998

- Treasurer: collected dues; presented weekly reports
- Featured artist in local area shows

American Field Service Member	1996-1997

- Treasurer/Secretary: collected dues; took minutes at weekly meetings; gave weekly treasury reports

---

To Do:

If you have only a few activities and honors, combine them into one listing here.

_____

_____

_____

_____

Workshops, Seminars, and Related Programs

Furthering your knowledge in a special area of interest is a valuable experience. Workshops, seminars, summer and weekend programs, and special projects are good ways to learn more about a subject and help you decide if a field interests you as a career. Specialized training is offered in such areas as sports, computers, writing, languages, drafting, music, theater, and many others. Ask your teachers, counselors, coaches, and school activity sponsors about these opportunities. Special projects are another good way to explore areas of interest. You could, for example, do a research or marketing project for the family business or complete a special school project.

Be sure to add these additional learning experiences to your resume. Employers and colleges will appreciate knowing that you furthered your knowledge and had the initiative and desire to do so. Here are some examples of how to present this information:

WORKSHOPS AND SEMINARS

Workshop on Peer Mediation, James Madison High School, Dallas, TX
    2 days, Fall 1998

Writers' Workshop, Susquehanna University, Roscoe, TX
    2 weeks, Summer 1998

Women in the Workplace, Park School, Waco, TX
    1 day, Fall 1997

Peabody Institute, Dallas, TX
    Private piano study, 1996 to present

Special Programs

Outward Bound Program, Toronto, Canada	Spring 1998
Kanagawa Lacrosse Exchange to Japan	Summer 1997

SPECIAL PROJECTS

Research project on F. Scott Fitzgerald's life and works	1998
Entry in Maryland Bridge-Building Contest	1997
Research project on use of language in *A Clockwork Orange*	1997

To Do:

List workshops and seminars that you have attended. Include the sponsoring organization's name and the years you attended.

_____

_____

_____

_____

_____

_____

List any summer and weekend programs you have attended. Include the names of notable instructors if appropriate. Write down the years attended.

_____

_____

_____

_____

_____

_____

_____

List your special projects, along with the dates you completed them.

_____

_____

_____

_____

_____

Internships, Work-Study Programs, and Tech Prep Programs

Combining classroom and hands-on training through an internship, work-study program, or tech prep program helps you get solid work experience. To find out if these programs are for you, talk with your teachers and counselors about your interests.

On your resume, describe your participation in such a program fully. Include relevant courses, the company for which you worked, your title, participation dates, and areas of responsibility. If you received certification through the program (such as in CPR or cosmetology), be sure to list that information. With this experience and education on your resume, you will be ready for additional training and be very employable in the field.

Internships

An internship can give you invaluable experience now and help you get a job later. Some fields in which you can find internships are business, health care, human services, radio and television, advertising, government, public relations, magazine and book publishing, and performing and fine arts. An internship should be presented just like a job on your resume:

Geriatric Assistant—Sunrise Assisted Living Corp. Chicago, IL   Summer 1998
- Helped the 25 residents of this assisted living home
- Assisted with daily living needs and activities

Work-Study Programs

In a work-study program, you will spend part of your day taking regular courses and part of your day at a job. This experience gives you good exposure to the workplace before graduation. You are usually paid for work-study jobs. A position held through a work-study program should be presented like a job on your resume:

U.S. Army Corps of Engineers, Sugarland, TX   Spring 1998
  Field Technician. Field sampling and lab testing for government and commercial customers. Hands-on experience in laboratory testing facility. Familiar with OSHA, DNR, and EPA environmental compliance regulations for hazardous materials handling and construction.

Tech Prep Programs

A tech prep program is a specialized curriculum consisting of both classes and employment or an internship in a particular field, such as automotive technology, computer graphics and design, accounting, or paralegal work. By completing a tech prep program, you are prepared for an occupation or additional education in that field. Here are examples of tech prep programs presented on resumes:

Allied Health Tech Prep Program—Direct Patient Care

Major Courses

Emergency Medical Technology	Anatomy
Physiology	Kinesiology
Fitness Evaluations	Direct Care Services

Meridian Healthcare, Cheyenne Wells, CO   Spring 1998

Geriatric Technician. Skills developed include patient care, activity planning, family and physician communications.

Certificates

CPR and First Aid, American Red Cross

Culinary Arts and Restaurant Management

Major Courses

Restaurant Management	Food Preparation and Baking
Purchasing	Computerized Inventory Control
Menu Planning	Sanitation

Olde Philadelphia Inn, Pine Busk, NY   January 1998– present

Banquet Assistant. Skilled in food preparation for banquets and full-service meals. Assist chef with menu planning, buying, and inventory control. Maintain sanitation in kitchen.

Certification: New York State Sanitation Certification

Cosmetology

Major Courses

Completed 1,500 hours theoretical and clinical courses in styling and aesthetician training, including Chemistry, Dermatology, Anatomy, Physiology, and Sanitation.

Eastern Salon, Los Alamitos, CA   Spring 1998

Stylist and Assistant Aesthetician. Trained and experienced in hair styling, customer service, and sales. Familiar with inventory management, product knowledge, and skin care consultation. Knowledgeable about dermatology, cosmetology, and general shop standards.

License: Passed the State of California Board Examination   April 1998

Automotive Technology

Major Courses

Instruction and training in all aspects of automobile operation and service.

Diagnostic Equipment   Computerized Automotive System Simulators
Estimating   Parts Reference and Selection

Ridgeway Motors, Redondo Beach, CA   Spring 1998-present
Mechanic's Assistant
♦ Skilled with diagnosis and repair of automotive systems.
♦ Skilled in estimating, parts reference, buying, and selection.
♦ Utilize computerized automotive systems in the shop and classroom.

Computer Information Technology

Major Courses

Extensive hands-on lab experience on IBM systems and Novell Network and BASIC, RPG, and C programming languages.

Microsoft Office Suite   Windows 95 Systems Training
Lotus 1-2-3   Harvard Graphics

Brown & Brown, Colorado Springs, CO   Summer 1998
Computer Technician
• Installed, repaired, and troubleshot PC systems for stand-alone and networked systems.
• Installed and upgraded software programs, including Windows 95.
• Installed Internet browsers, set up ISPs, and assisted users with new systems.

Bureau of Census, Fruita, CO   Summer 1997
Computer Programmer
• Performed programming in C language, primarily to assist with upgrading programs for the Year 2000 Census.
• Assisted with user questions.

Computer-Aided Drafting and Design

Major Courses

Structural Drafting and Design	Civil Drafting	AutoCAD
Electromechanical Drafting	Architectural Design	Blueprint Reading
Five courses in Advanced Math and Science		

CAD Operator   Summer 1998-Spring 1999
   Rogers Contractors, Lansing, MI
   • Utilized AutoCAD 14 to produce blueprints for civil engineering, including real property, roads, landscaping, irrigation, and buildings.
   • Assisted with copying blueprints and organizing customer presentations.

Computer Graphics and Design

Major Courses

Copy and Art Preparation	Advertising and Packaging
Portfolio Development	Graphic Communication
Scanning and Photoshop II	Adobe Illustrator

Stockton Graphics, Wilmington, NC   Summer 1998-present
Computer Graphics Assistant
   ♦ Utilize PC system with Microsoft Office, Adobe, PowerPoint, and scanning systems.
   ♦ Produce graphics for overheads, brochures, letterhead, and Web sites.
   ♦ Familiar with HTML programming and integration of jpg and psd graphic files.

Construction Technology—Plumbing and HVAC

Major Courses

Hand and Power Tools	Foundation Layout	Electrical Theory
Blueprint Reading	Strength and Materials	Job Estimating

Anderson Plumbing, Schenectady, NY   Fall 1998-present
   Plumber's Assistant
   • Install and maintain water supply systems, waste removal systems, fixtures, and gas appliances for residential homes.

Madison Contractors, Saratoga Springs, NY   Summers, 1997 and 1998
   HVAC Intern/Project Assistant for new HVAC plant installation at University of Maryland Baltimore County campus.
   • Assisted with construction, tear-out, and installation of large plant.
   • Familiar with safety provisions and digital controls.
   • Learned the basics for installation of central air, heat pumps, oil furnaces, and light commercial units.

Electronics

Major Courses

Troubleshooting Techniques	Electronic Circuits
Analog and Digital Electronics	Power Supplies
Testing Equipment and Techniques	Microprocessor Circuits

West Electric, Sarasota, FL   Spring 1998-present
Intern
- Perform bench work repair and assist with manufacturing plant field visits.
- Use knowledge of power supplies, amplifiers, oscillators, and transceivers.
- Skilled with test equipment.

Legal Assistant/Paralegal Studies

Major Courses

Legal Research Methods–Lexis/Nexis	Principles of Law
Computerized Document Control	Legal Institutions

Legal Assistant. Law Offices of Tom Graham, Missoula, MT   Summer 1998
Utilized PC to word process correspondence, pleadings, and memoranda. Scheduled appointments. Became familiar with legal formats, computer systems, court calendar, and case management systems.

Accounting

Major Courses

Debits and Credits	Microsoft Money
Accounting I & II	Economics
Banking	Finance

Mark Morrison, CPA, Atlanta, GA   Spring and Summer 1998
Accounting Assistant. Assisted with compiling tax returns and inputting information for individual clients and small businesses. Utilized QuickBooks and Microsoft Money. Scheduled appointments.

Secretarial/Office Automation

Major Courses
Computers: Microsoft Suite—Word 7, Excel, PowerPoint
Systems and Administration   Communications Skills

Landmark Insurance, Old Westbury, NY   Spring 1998-present
Secretary to Insurance Broker. Assist with preparation of correspondence, policies, and presentations. Utilize Microsoft Word 7.0, Excel, and Publisher. Manage e-mail and voice mail messages. Input data into database in Access.

To Do:

List your internship, work-study, and tech prep positions. Include the company names, your job titles, dates, and areas of responsibility. If you were in training most of the time, list the types of training you received.

_____

_____

_____

_____

_____

_____

_____

_____

_____

List the major courses that supported your concentration.

_____

_____

_____

_____

If you completed a special project, write about the project here.

_____

_____

_____

_____

_____

List any certificates or licenses received.

_____

_____

_____

_____

Service-Learning and Volunteer Experiences

Some high schools require service learning to graduate. You can find out about service-learning opportunities through your school guidance counselor and service-learning coordinator. You can seek volunteer work on your own if your school does not require service learning.

If you have an area of interest (for example, music, social work, animal care, psychology, or business), then apply for service-learning positions in that field. Remember that volunteers can be a valuable help to an organization. Add the description of your experience to your resume like a paid job. Study the examples that follow.

Student's interest is in horses and special education:

TAP'S HORSE FARM, Boulder, CO   Summers 1996, 1997
  Walker—Assisted with training horses. Exercised and groomed animals. Cleaned stalls. Ran errands for staff. Walked horses for developmentally disabled young riders; ensured their safety and enjoyment of the experience.

Student's interest is in human services and psychology:

Volunteer, Taos Emergency Food Ministries, Taos, NM
School Years, 1995-1998
   ♦ Assisted with activities of nonprofit service organization, including office duties, inventory, direct mail distribution, and fund-raising
   ♦ Responded to telephone inquiries regarding needs and services

Student's interest is in music education and performance:

VOLUNTEER ACTIVITIES
   Steel drum musician performing at schools, retirement centers, and private parties, 1997-present
   Play piano at El Paso Methodist Church Services, 1996-present
   Assisted the music program for Vacation Bible School at El Paso United Methodist Church, 1995-1996

Student's interest is in early childhood education and teaching:

Camp Counselor, Spring Blossom Playground, Red Bluff, CA   Summer 1998
Supervised play and lunch. Accompanied day trips for children aged four to ten.

Student's interest is in creative writing and poetry:

Cohost of *Function at the Junction*, a twice-monthly local poetry reading, Chanute, KS, 1998.

Student's interest is in the health-care field, especially geriatric:

Hospital Volunteer, Glendale Hospital, Glendale, CA   Summer 1998
Responsible for transporting wheelchair-bound patients, handling basic medical tasks, answering phones, and filing papers in hospital recovery room.

Volunteer, Pasadena Manor Nursing Home, Pasadena, CA   Summer 1997
Helped organize and run senior activities.

To Do:

List the name of the companies or organizations where you did service learning and volunteer work. Include the dates.

_____

_____

_____

_____

_____

What was your title for each position?

_____

_____

_____

_____

Describe your duties for each position.

_____

_____

_____

_____

_____

_____

_____

If you learned something new about a certain field of work or industry, write that here.

_____

_____

_____

_____

_____

_____

_____

_____

Work Experience

Your work experience will demonstrate to potential employers, colleges, and everyone who sees your resume the following:

- ✉ Type of skills and industry experience

- ✉ Level of responsibility and capability

- ✉ Customer and product information

- ✉ Ability to communicate and work with the public

- ✉ Ability to handle multiple tasks (academics, activities, job)

- ✉ Interest in helping pay for personal expenses (personal motivation and responsibility)

Here are examples of how to present work experience on your resume:

NOPOLIS FAMILY, Colorado Springs, CO   Summers, 1997, 1998
    Nanny. Responsible for the daily activities, safety, and care of two children, ages 8 and 10. Managed a busy schedule consisting of swim team, parties, and day trips, in cooperation with professional parents.

YAGER'S BAGELS, Utica, NY   1996-present
    Bagel Prep/Cashier. Under tight production schedules, prepare bagel sandwiches for up to 150 customers per day. Use proper health and safety precautions. Provide customer services and operate cash register.

Teacher's Aide, Vail Mountain School, Vail, CO   1997
  - Assisted teachers with after-school activities of 35 second-grade students.
  - Planned activities and program materials.
  - Provided one-on-one and group instruction and stories.
  - Created a mini-theater activity involving student actors using their imaginative ideas for the play.

CROSS-COUNTRY INSURANCE, Springfield, IL   Summer 1998
Office Assistant. Utilized PC with Windows and Word 7.0 to produce correspondence and policyholder reports. Answered telephones, screened calls, and took detailed messages. Researched customer inquiries.

GREENE'S AUTO PARTS, Columbus, OH   Part-time, 1996-present
Delivery Person. Prepare orders, developed route, and deliver parts based on faxed and telephone orders. Meet or exceed quota of 20-30 deliveries per day. Provide customer service and research problems.

RETAIL CLERK. 7-ELEVEN STORES, Walsenburg, CO   January 1997-present
  - Responsible for store maintenance, customer service, cash management.
  - Prepare weekly invoice orders.
  - Train new employees.

To Do:

List your part-time and full-time positions here. Include the name of each employer, the title of your position, and employment dates.

_____

_____

_____

_____

_____

_____

_____

_____

_____

_____

_____

_____

_____

_____

List your main responsibilities for each job.

_____

_____

_____

_____

_____

_____

_____

_____

_____

_____

_____

_____

Include the skills you used on the job. Try to use any key words that would be appropriate for the employer.

_____

_____

_____

_____

_____

_____

_____

_____

_____

_____

_____

_____

_____

_____

_____

_____

_____

_____

_____

_____

_____

Describing Your Skills

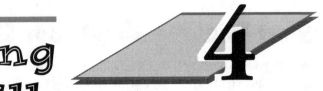

"Cool skill, Rob! But is it one employers want?"

Successfully applying for a job or internship with a targeted resume requires that

- ✉ You know what your skills are.

- ✉ You can communicate your skills in writing.

- ✉ You are able to speak effectively about them.

As explained in Chapter 2, your targeted resume includes two main parts: one describing your skills and one listing your background. In the last chapter, you answered questions that will help you write the second part of your resume. In this chapter, you will work on describing your skills for the first part. Why create the first part (Skills sections) *after* the second part (Background and Experience sections)? By listing your courses, activities, honors, and jobs, it will be easier to identify the skills you've developed.

Start Thinking About Your Skills

When you look at activities and honors, you can often guess what the students' best skills are, can't you? Here are two examples:

> **HONORS**
> Region 81 Champion Team Roper, 1998
> Rodeo State Finalist (Calf Roping and Team Roping), 1997, 1998
> Lone Star Farmer, 1997
> Member, 4-H Club—raised show lambs

This student is a cowboy who possesses skills to work with animals, work on a ranch, or work in agriculture. Related skills are dependability, physical strength, and coordination.

> **Honors**
> ♦ Honored by Bloomsburg Parks & Recreation Association for outstanding service for volunteerism for early childhood after-school program, 1997-1998
> ♦ Received Third Place, Candid Photography Contest, *Washington Post*, May 1997
> ♦ Received a certificate for participation in children's programs, Bethany Baptist Church, 1997

This student likes working with kids. Photography is another interest. The student's skills focus on education, recreation, and photography.

A *skill* is the ability to do something well (such as work with computers or grow a garden). A skill can also be part of your personality (such as being organized, articulate, or competitive).

When you analyze your honors, activities, courses, internships, and work experience, what do you see? Is there a common thread of skills and interests? Are there certain things you do well and enjoy? If so, keep working on them. Add to the list as much as you can. That will make you marketable to an employer.

Employers value skills applicable to specific jobs but also look at the skills that make you who you are. No matter what the industry, employers want workers who are willing to learn; have good reading, writing, and math skills; are good listeners and speakers; think creatively; solve problems; set goals; are motivated; and work well in a team. Look for ways to present skills such as these on your resume.

Students on the debate team possess skills in research, public speaking, and working under pressure.

Participating in sports develops skills in teamwork, coordination, perseverance, and strategic thinking.

The Importance of Key Words

As mentioned in Chapter 2, key words reflect the skills needed for a job. These key words often appear in classified ads. Examples of key words are *writing ability, computer knowledge, planning skills,* and a *customer service orientation.* The closer your skills match the desired skills, the better your chance of landing an interview.

Scanning is another reason to include key words on your resume. Scanning is new technology for reviewing resumes by Optical Character Readers (OCRs). The scanner is set up to find key words. If your resume does not contain the key words for a certain position, you will not be considered.

If your resume has many key words for a specific job (such as Emily's targeted resumes in Chapter 2), the scanner will rate you highly. You may be called for an interview.

Scanning is used by large companies to pinpoint the most qualified applicants. Scanning saves time for employers because they can focus on candidates with the right skills. Employers don't have to read every resume that crosses their desks.

Recognizing Your Skills

You need to relate the skills you have gained from your courses, activities, workshops, and positions so that employers see at a glance what you can do for them. Depending on the job, you can *slant* the same skills in different ways. For example, Emily's skills from the debate team went under Communications Skills when applying for an internship with Congress and under Interpretation Skills for a National Parks position. Another option is to have one Summary of Skills section without subheadings.

CASE STUDY

How Emily Grouped Her Skills

As described in Chapter 2, Emily's targeted resumes listed her relevant skills at the top. She used key words that were appropriate to the jobs she wanted.

When applying for the Kings Canyon position, she knew that trail workers did a lot of hard work and that honors would not be important. Here's how Emily organized her background into groups of skills important for a National Parks volunteer job:

OBJECTIVE: Trail Worker, Volunteer-in-Parks, Kings Canyon, California

SUMMARY OF RELEVANT SKILLS AND EXPERIENCE

Outdoor Leadership Experience

National Outdoor Leadership School, Lander, WY, Summer 1997
Graduated Rocky Mountain Horsepacking course involving one week of ranch experience and two weeks of backcountry travel in the Wind River range. Trained in minimum impact camping, backpacking, and horsepacking. Emphasis on backcountry leadership skills necessary to lead future personal expeditions: safety and judgment, leadership and teamwork, outdoor skills, environmental ethics, and horse handling and packing skills.

Interpretation Skills

Internship, Haleakala National Park, Maui, HI, Fall 1997
Interpretation at high-volume visitor center and development of special projects, including park displays and 20-minute naturalist visitor programs. Hiked inside the volcano six miles.
High School Public Speaking
Experienced researcher and writer in high school and community publications. Four years' experience in theater and debate competitions.

Sports and Athletic Experience

Member, varsity field hockey team, 1996
Enjoy hiking, backpacking, and camping
Physically fit

Key words

Relevant experience
identifiable
at a glance

TIP BEFORE ASSUMING THAT YOU DON'T POSSESS THE SKILLS NEEDED FOR A PARTICULAR JOB, BE SURE TO LOOK CLOSELY AT YOUR BACKGROUND AND ABILITIES. OFTEN YOU WILL HAVE A FEW SKILLS THAT ARE RELAVANT TO THE JOB. THINK CREATIVELY!

Emily wrote another targeted resume that was completely different because it was directed toward a Congressional or professional job. Her skills section highlighted writing, research, communications, and computers, as shown next.

OBJECTIVE: Internship with a nonprofit association or legislative office.

SUMMARY OF RELEVANT SKILLS AND EXPERIENCE

Writing and Research Experience

Skilled researcher of political and policy issues with debate league. Course emphasis has been on English and writing. Editor of the *Phoenix* literary/art publication. Published poetry in school, community, and college literary publications. Attended two college writing workshops for critical thinking and writing.

Key words

Communications Skills

Four years in theater with the lead in a popular comedy. Selected for highly competitive Shakespeare workshop. National competitor in debate competitions. Leadership training. Invited to read poetry at public venues with students and established poets.

Computer Skills

Experience with PCs and Macintosh; Windows 95, Microsoft Office, Word 7.0, WordPerfect 6.1, Internet; keyboard over 45 wpm.

Summarizing Your Skills

Selling your skills to a potential employer is important. The hiring manager will review your resume for a very short time (only 3 to 10 seconds). Make sure the individual sees that you have the skills to do the job. Listing a Summary of Skills at the top is a smart way to emphasize your abilities. The examples that follow show how you can highlight skills developed through school and work. The first bullets are *hard skills* (facts), and the last bullet in each example is a *soft skill* (personal quality).

TIP NOTICE HOW COURSES AND ACTIVITIES HAVE BEEN TURNED INTO SKILLS THAT EMPLOYERS VALUE. THE SAME CAN BE TRUE FOR YOU. EVEN IF YOU DON'T HAVE PAID WORK EXPERIENCE, YOU CAN PRESENT MANY SKILLS ON YOUR RESUME. DO YOU POSSESS ANY SKILLS SIMILAR TO THOSE IN THE FOLLOWING EXAMPLES?

Objective: Editorial Assistant

Summary of Skills

❖ Proofread and edit 8-page newsletter monthly
❖ Follow *The Chicago Manual of Style* for editorial consistency
❖ Review and coordinate article submissions by students
❖ Select photographs and write captions
❖ Effective team member in publishing group

Objective: Secretary/Office Assistant

Summary of Skills

■ PC experience using Word 6.0 (3 years)
■ Keyboarding speed 55 words per minute
■ Proofreading skills and course work in business communications
■ Received A's in all business technology and administrative courses
■ Organized, efficient, and able to handle pressure

Objective: Bench Technician

Summary of Skills

● Four years of experience working with PCs in computer laboratory and personal system
● Skilled with troubleshooting PC hardware and software
● Course work and self-study in Windows 3.0 and Windows 95 systems
● Experienced in installing and upgrading software, back-ups, and file management
● Technically adept and enjoy reading computer manuals and schematics

Objective: Telemarketer/Inside Sales

Summary of Skills

◆ Three years in theater, both drama and musicals, with leading roles
◆ Received A's and B's in all public speaking and communications courses
◆ Three years of experience in retail sales with extensive customer communications
◆ Articulate, outgoing, and persuasive

An internship at an advertising agency helps develop skills in proofreading, oral and written communication, and client services.

To Do:

List skills you have gained through courses, internships, and vocational training.

_____

_____

_____

_____

List skills you have gained through extracurricular activities and sports.

_____

_____

_____

_____

List skills you have gained through volunteer and work experiences.

_____

_____

_____

_____

List skills you have gained through hobbies, self-study, and interests outside school.

_____

_____

_____

_____

Give each skill in the lists above a number, with *1* representing your best skill. This skills list will be helpful in writing the Skills section for your targeted resume, writing cover letters, and describing yourself in interviews.

Understanding Your Soft Skills

As mentioned in the previous section, you should list soft skills on your resume. You possess many soft skills. Describing your soft skills is a good way to make yourself more appealing in the job market.

Think of soft skills as part of who you are and how you deal with situations. If you need help thinking about your soft skills, consider what your teachers and coaches would say about you. Soft skills can be divided into two categories, as listed here:

Adaptive skills, which help you adapt to many situations. Examples of adaptive skills are

- [x] Enthusiasm
- [x] Honesty
- [x] Maturity

- [x] Physical strength and stamina
- [x] Fast learning
- [x] Sincerity

☒ Patience

☒ Competitiveness

☒ Getting along with teammates

☒ Hard working

Transferable skills, which are general skills that can be used in many jobs. Examples of transferable skills include

☒ Finishing assignments on time

☒ Staying organized

☒ Working with people

☒ Following instructions

☒ Dependability

☒ Paying attention to detail

☒ Flexibility

☒ Speaking before groups

☒ Ability to handle many projects at once

☒ Leading a club

☒ Writing clearly

☒ Expressing yourself through art, music, dance, writing

Some skills can fit into either group. For example, paying attention to detail is a way that you function from day-to-day as well as being a skill that can be used in many jobs. Don't worry about the words *adaptive* and *transferable*— just remember to value your soft skills and include them on your resume.

Performing in a school play improves many soft skills, including teamwork, public speaking, and creative expression.

To Do:

Make a list of soft skills you possess. If you've already listed soft skills in your answers earlier, try to think of a few more.

_____

_____

_____

_____

Listing Your Technical Skills

Specific technical skills can help you get a job. Being extremely clear about technical skills is important. A potential employer will appreciate seeing this section neatly organized with the equipment name and type listed.

Keep your technical skills up-to-date. For example, if you list Windows 3.0 when Windows 98 is in use, you may not get considered. Self-study and training courses will keep you current with the latest technology. Virtually every resume in today's job market should include a Computer or Technical Skills section. Here are some samples of this section:

Computer Skills

Macintosh:	Microsoft Word (6 years)
PC:	Windows 98, Word, WordPerfect
Internet:	Research, e-mail, Netscape, and Explorer

Technical and Computer Skills
PC: Windows, WordPerfect 6.1, Internet
Macintosh: Mini-CAD 5.02

Summary of Skills
Word Processing: Word 7.0, WordPerfect 6.1
Desktop Publishing: PageMaker (proficient), Quark (self-study)
Scanning: Photographs and graphics for print publication
Internet: HTML and basic Web site development

Electronic Music

Home Studio	Digital Sampler ASR 10; Denon 3-head, 2-track tape deck; NAD 1600 preamp; Nakamichi STASIS amp; Infinity Ref, Series II; PC with Cakewalk, Mackie 24x8, Alesis Adat; Tascam DAT MK30II
Performance	53-keyboard, electric bass, various acoustic instruments
Recordings	Puddle–demo
Interests	Original music composition–digital and acoustic recording
Memberships	Washington Area Music Association

To Do:

List your computer and technology-related skills.

_____

_____

_____

_____

The Big Picture

Now that you've thought about and listed your specific skills, complete the following information to gain a better sense of their importance.

To Do:

List three things that would make you a good employee.

1. _____

_____

2. _____

_____

3. _____

_____

How do you think a potential employer would view you and your skills?

_____

_____

_____

_____

Which skills would you like to develop or improve, and why?

_____

_____

_____

_____

How can you develop these skills?

_____

_____

_____

_____

Which skills would you like to use most in a job, and why?

_____

_____

_____

_____

Formatting Your Resume 5

"I tattooed my resume here. My references are only available on request since I have to take off my shirt."

Keeping the reader's attention focused on your resume is a challenge. The average length for a resume review is 3 to 10 seconds. You can increase that time if your resume is attractively formatted, well-organized, and error-free. If your resume looks unpolished, disorganized, or contains grammar and spelling mistakes, it makes a negative impression and will end up in the nearest recycling bin.

Definitions for Resume Layout

A good layout can enhance your resume's content. An employer's eye will go to the top and center of the page, so your contact information should be in that position. Putting other important details near the top (such as a Skills section) ensures that they will get read. Information at the bottom may not get close scrutiny. Finally, by making resume headings a large, consistently placed element, an employer can find relevant information without confusion.

The following terms will help you understand the elements that create your resume's look and feel. Experiment with type font, style, and size to get a look you like and to make your resume fit one page. Avoid using too many type faces and type styles.

Type Font

Many type fonts are available on a personal computer. A few popular fonts are Times, Arial, Bookman, and Baskerville. Each type font conveys a different feel and image.

Times. This type is very traditional and looks like book type. It is very easy to read and conservative. Times has *serifs*, a French word for edges on the type. Here is part of a resume in Times:

EDUCATION

Martin High School, Restaurant Management Program, Sacramento, CA; graduated May 1998

Major Courses
Restaurant Management   Food Preparation and Baking
Purchasing   Computerized Inventory Control

Arial. This type is more contemporary and is a *sans serif* font. That means it does not have the little edges on the type (without serifs). It is very clean, bold, and rather assertive, as you see in the following example:

EXPERIENCE

Jonelle's Lodge, Sacramento, CA   January 1997–Present
Chef's Assistant. Assist with food preparation for banquets (25 to 250 guests) and full-service meals. Assist chef with menu planning, buying, and inventory control.

Martin High School Cafeteria   Academic years 1996, 1997
Chef's Assistant. Assisted cooks with food preparation. Devised improved serving methods for students. Maintained salad bar. Worked as server and dishwasher as needed.

Bookman. This type is a serif font and has a graphic look. The type is wide and takes up more room than the two fonts above. The bold is very dark. This font looks more distinctive than Times. Study the following example:

SKILLS and QUALIFICATIONS

- Food preparation, sanitation, menu development and implementation, promotional sales, catering, banquet preparation and service, dining room service, bakeshop production

- Hold California State Sanitation Certification

- Good communication skills; bilingual Spanish/English

Baskerville. This type is a serif font. It is very classy. It is a thin font and not as bold as the others. But it has a regal look. This font makes a resume stand out, as the following sample shows:

EDUCATION

Nottingham High School, Orlando, FL

Allied Health Tech Prep Program–Direct Patient Care. Graduated May 1998.
GPA 3.963   Rank 2/273

Selected courses: Medical Terminology; Anatomy and Physiology; Biology; Chemistry; Psychology; Spanish I, II, III

Type Style

Bold, *italics*, ***bold italics***, ALL CAPS, and SMALL CAPS are type styles. Be consistent with the use of type style. For example, if you use bold and all caps for one job title, use bold and all caps for every job title. If you use italics for your position titles, then you need to do this each time.

Bold. Bold can be used to highlight major headings, school and employer names, titles of positions, and information that you want to stand out:

Glenelg Country School, Glenelg, MD

Italics. It is customary to type Latin words in italics, such as magna cum laude and names of fraternities or sororities. Italic type is hard to read, so use it sparingly.

Graduated summa cum laude, 1998

Bold italics. The bold italics is useful for a secondary heading. A typical use for bold italics would be the titles of positions:

Hostess, Edison Assisted Living Center

ALL CAPS. Usually the major headings are in all caps. Sometimes employers' names and your high school name can be in all caps.

EDUCATION

COMMUNITY SERVICE

COMPUTER SKILLS

SMALL CAPS. This is another way to emphasize titles, names, and section headings:

SUSAN M. GOWER

EDUCATION

WORK EXPERIENCE

Type Size

Typically 11-point type is used for most resumes; 10 point is acceptable if you need to fit a great deal of information on one page. You might want to set your name in 14-point type so it stands out. The headings for your resume could be in 12 point for extra emphasis.

10-point type:

SPRINGBROOK HIGH SCHOOL, Orange, CA. Graduated June 1998
Marching Band, Pit Orchestra, and Jazz Band—all four years.
Junior ROTC— four years. Rank: Ensign. Assigned as Commander, senior year.

11-point type:

Bishop Noll High School, Butler, PA
Graduated June 1998
Trombonist in the Symphonic Band, 1994-1998
Treasurer of the Astronomy Club, 1995-1997

12-point type:

Computer Skills

14-point type:

BRIAN L. WEBER

TIP THIS CHAPTER CONTAINS FORMATTING GUIDELINES, NOT FORMATTING RULES. USE YOUR CREATIVITY TO ADAPT THESE GUIDELINES TO YOUR RESUME.

Layout

Layout is the overall design of the resume and includes element placement, element alignment, margins, and spacing. Be consistent with your layout. For example, be sure to use the same amount of spacing between each section of your resume.

Copyfitting

This means fitting your resume into a certain amount of space, usually one page. You can copyfit by adjusting the line spaces and changing the type size, type font, and margins. If your resume is five or ten lines over one page, you can copyfit the information into one page with spacing and type changes.

White Space

White space between and around sections throughout your resume makes it easy on the eyes. Too much white space causes a resume to look skimpy; too little makes it look busy and cluttered. Use your judgment to obtain an easy-to-read mix of words and white space.

Bullets

Paragraphs can be written in block style or with bullets to highlight every sentence, as you see in the following samples:

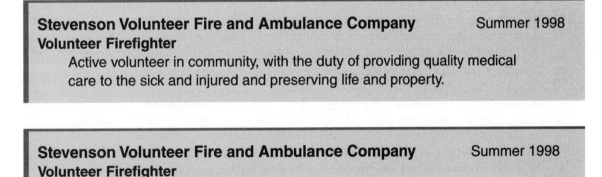

Stevenson Volunteer Fire and Ambulance Company   Summer 1998
Volunteer Firefighter
      Active volunteer in community, with the duty of providing quality medical care to the sick and injured and preserving life and property.

Stevenson Volunteer Fire and Ambulance Company   Summer 1998
Volunteer Firefighter

  o Active volunteer in community
  o Provide quality medical care to the sick and injured
  o Preserve life and property

Selecting Your Favorite Format

Here are four resume format examples: traditional, contemporary, graphic, and scannable. Each conveys a different feel and serves a different purpose.

Traditional

A traditional-style resume uses Times or other serif type that is easy to read.

TERRY R. RICHARDS

25 Esposito Lane
Bakersfield, California 90000
(555) 555-5555

Objective

Sales Associate—Outdoor Recreation Retail

Skills & Knowledge

- Knowledge and experience in outdoor recreation and parks.
- Firsthand experience with trail construction tools and equipment.
- Communication and instruction skills in use of equipment, tools, and methods.
- Experienced in crew living and camping in the backcountry for a total of 20 months.
- Knowledge of environmental programs and importance of minimum impact camping.

Work Experience

CALIFORNIA CONSERVATION CORPS

CORPS MEMBER/TRAIL WORKER (PAID POSITION)   Summer 1998

KLAMATH NATIONAL FOREST, SHASTA TRINITY NATIONAL FOREST, KINGS CANYON NATIONAL PARK

- Maintained trails, constructed rock work, and rehabilitated damaged meadows.
- Constructed causeway, single and multitier rockwall, inside and outside drains and wash pans over slickrock and through trail sections that have undergone erosion and water damage.
- Camp life: Lived and worked with 18 people in the crew for four months in the backcountry. Shared kitchen patrol duties; relocated camp frequently; hiked trail and cross-country tours for as far as 20 miles round-trip; attended four classes per week in related subjects.
- Equipment: Crosscuts (saw), picks, pulawskis, sledge hammers, chinking hammers, shovels, loppers, pinonjars, dirt buckets, blasting equipment.

SALMON RESTORATION SPECIALIST (PAID POSITION)   April 1997—April 1998

SALMON RESTORATION PROJECTS/FISHERIES AND OIL RECYCLING EDUCATION

- Constructed salmon restoration sites.
- Utilized natural materials to improve the salmon habitat.
- Repaired damaged sections of riparian zones.

Special Skills & Awards

- Presentations concerning environmental effects of oil recycling, 1998.
- Corps Member of the Month, March 1998.

Education & Training

Bakersfield High School, Bakersfield, California—Expect to graduate May 1999.

Other Training: How to Pack for the Backcountry, 3/98, 20 hours; Minimum Impact Camping, 4/98, 20 hours; Basic First Aid, 5/98, 10 hours; River Rescue, 6/98, 8 hours.

Other Interests

Member of soccer team (goalkeeper). Also enjoy basketball, mountain biking, photography (35mm), in addition to camping and hiking.

Contemporary

Give your resume a contemporary look by using Arial or other sans serif type that is bold and dynamic.

ANDY G. TABORI
108 Cliff Avenue
Reno, NV 99999
(555) 555-0000

OBJECTIVE	Seeking an internship in the field of culinary arts and the hospitality industry.
EDUCATION	Reno High School, Reno, NV. Expect to graduate May 1999

Culinary Arts and Restaurant Management Program
Major Courses:

Restaurant Management	Food Preparation and Baking
Purchasing	Menu Planning
Computerized Inventory Control	Sanitation

SKILLS	o Food Preparation, Sanitation, Menu Development and Implementation, Promotional Sales, Catering, Banquet Preparation and Service, Dining Room Service, Bakeshop Production
	o Hold California State Sanitation Certification
	o Good communication skills; bilingual Spanish/English
	o Computer literate (PC and Mac)

EXPERIENCE	**Reno High School Cafeteria** 1998-current
	Cafeteria Cook. Assist cooks with food preparation; maintain salad bar; work as server and dishwasher as needed.
	Kingsways Inn, Reno, NV Summer 1998
	Banquet Assistant. Assisted with food preparation for banquets and full-service meals. Assisted chef with menu planning, buying, and inventory control. Maintained sanitation in kitchen.
	St. Andrew's Catholic Church, Reno, NV Summer 1997
	Handyman. Performed grounds maintenance and janitorial duties.

COMPUTER SKILLS	Windows, Printshop Deluxe, Internet
INTERESTS	Cooking, camping, skiing, swimming, and fishing

Professional and personal references available on request

Graphic

A graphic resume can make use of lines, shadows, borders, and graphics. Suggested type fonts: Arial, Book Antiqua, or an unusual but readable type like Biffo and Gills Sans, below.

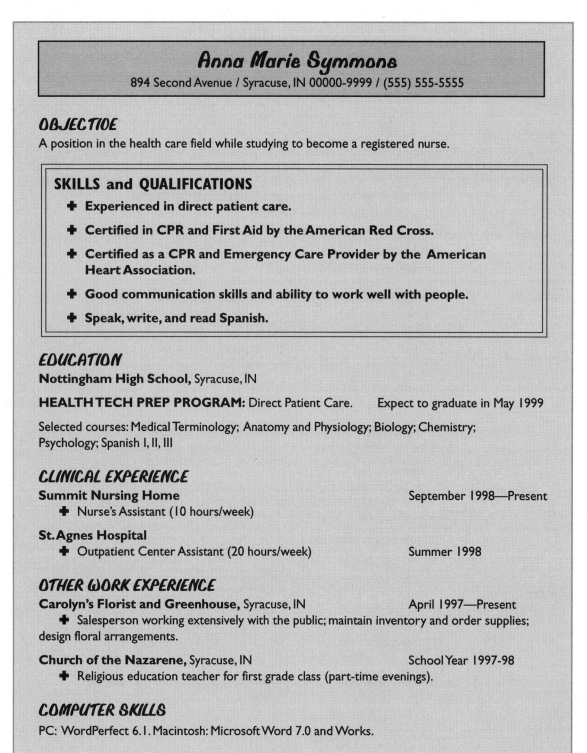

Anna Marie Symmons
894 Second Avenue / Syracuse, IN 00000-9999 / (555) 555-5555

OBJECTIVE

A position in the health care field while studying to become a registered nurse.

SKILLS and QUALIFICATIONS

+ **Experienced in direct patient care.**

+ **Certified in CPR and First Aid by the American Red Cross.**

+ **Certified as a CPR and Emergency Care Provider by the American Heart Association.**

+ **Good communication skills and ability to work well with people.**

+ **Speak, write, and read Spanish.**

EDUCATION

Nottingham High School, Syracuse, IN

HEALTH TECH PREP PROGRAM: Direct Patient Care.   Expect to graduate in May 1999

Selected courses: Medical Terminology; Anatomy and Physiology; Biology; Chemistry; Psychology; Spanish I, II, III

CLINICAL EXPERIENCE

Summit Nursing Home   September 1998—Present
  + Nurse's Assistant (10 hours/week)

St. Agnes Hospital
  + Outpatient Center Assistant (20 hours/week)   Summer 1998

OTHER WORK EXPERIENCE

Carolyn's Florist and Greenhouse, Syracuse, IN   April 1997—Present
  + Salesperson working extensively with the public; maintain inventory and order supplies; design floral arrangements.

Church of the Nazarene, Syracuse, IN   School Year 1997-98
  + Religious education teacher for first grade class (part-time evenings).

COMPUTER SKILLS

PC: WordPerfect 6.1. Macintosh: Microsoft Word 7.0 and Works.

Scannable

A scannable resume contains sans serif type, little formatting, no italics, no bullets, and no underlining. This resume type must be easy for a scanner to read; 11-point type is preferable. Scanners can read two-page resumes almost as fast as one, so you don't have to limit yourself to one page.

TERRY R. RICHARDS
Esposito Lane
Bakersfield, California 90000
(555) 555-5555

Objective
Sales Associate—Outdoor Recreation Retail

Skills & Knowledge
Knowledge and experience in outdoor recreation and parks.

Firsthand experience with trail construction tools and equipment.

Communication and instruction skills in use of equipment, tools, and methods.

Experienced in crew living and camping in the backcountry for a total of 20 months.

Knowledge of environmental programs and importance of minimum impact camping.

Work Experience
Summer 1998

CALIFORNIA CONSERVATION CORPS

Corps Member/Trail Worker (paid position)

Klamath National Forest, Shasta Trinity National Forest, Kings Canyon National Park

Maintained trails, constructed rock work, and rehabilitated damaged meadows. Constructed causeway, single and multitier rockwall, inside and outside drains and wash pans over slickrock and through trail sections that have undergone erosion and water damage.

Camp life: Lived and worked with 18 people in the crew for four months in the backcountry. Shared kitchen patrol duties; relocated camp frequently; hiked trail and cross-country tours for as far as 20 miles round-trip; attended four classes per week in related subjects.

Equipment: Crosscuts (saw), picks, pulawskis, sledge hammers, chinking hammers, shovels, loppers, pinonjars, dirt buckets, blasting equipment.

April 1997—April 1998

CALIFORNIA CONSERVATION CORPS

Salmon Restoration Specialist (paid position)

Salmon Restoration Projects/Fisheries and Oil Recycling Education

Constructed salmon restoration sites.

Utilized natural materials to improve the salmon habitat.

Repaired damaged sections of riparian zones.

Special Skills & Awards

Presentations concerning environmental effects of oil recycling, 1998.

Corps Member of the Month, March 1998.

Education & Training

Bakersfield High School, Bakersfield, California—Expect to graduate May 1999.

Other Training: How to Pack for the Backcountry, 3/98, 20 hours; Minimum Impact Camping, 4/98, 20 hours; Basic First Aid, 5/98, 10 hours; River Rescue, 6/98, 8 hours.

Other Interests

Member of Soccer Team (goalkeeper). Also enjoy basketball, mountain biking, photography (35mm), in addition to camping and hiking.

TIP WHEN YOU HAND OR MAIL A SCANNABLE RESUME TO EMPLOYERS, BE SURE TO STATE WHAT IT IS. SEND A NICELY FORMATTED RESUME ALONG WITH A CLEARLY LABELED SCANNABLE ONE.

To Do:

Which resume format do you like best: traditional, contemporary, graphic, or scannable? _____

Why? _____

_____

Which format will work best for your current objectives and why?

_____

_____

_____

Resume-Formatting Checklist

Here are pointers to keep in mind as you format your resume.

⊠ **Do not include your birth date, health status, or Social Security number.** Resumes usually should not include your birth date or photograph because Equal Employment Opportunity laws state that employers will not discriminate by age (too young or too old). Now that Web resumes are becoming popular, however, photographs are sometimes included to add personality to a resume.

Statements regarding health are not included, unless you're applying for a physical job. Your Social Security number should not be on your resume. Give it to an employer on your application if requested.

⊠ **State your objective carefully.** An objective is optional but helpful to include. Your objective should state the type of position you desire and may list the skills you want to use. Be careful not to limit yourself with an objective. For example, if you state that your objective is "entry-level clerical work," you may shut yourself out of more interesting jobs.

⊠ **Average resume length is one page.** The average length of a student resume is one page. If your resume is a few lines longer than one page, adjust your type size and margins to get it on a single sheet. If, however, you have a long list of employers, internships, awards, and activities, then write a two-page resume. Remember that you are selling yourself. If you have exceptional accomplishments as a high school student, then you deserve two pages.

With the new scanning technology, many applicants are not sticking to one page. The scanners can read two pages almost as fast as one. You can then include all the key words that the scanners need to rate your resume in the top ten percent. When your resume is scanned, it is often never seen by a hiring manager. The manager sees only the scanned data sheet of information.

✉ **Use preferred type sizes.** As mentioned earlier, use 10- or 11-point type for text; 12-point for headings; and 14-point for your name.

✉ **Make it error-free.** Refer to the dictionary and your grammar books as needed. Run the spell checker, but be aware that the spell checker won't catch all errors. Spell checkers and grammar checkers miss mistakes in dates, proper names, and titles. These tools cannot spot inconsistencies in format either.

Have a friend, teacher, or parent read your resume to make sure the grammar, punctuation, and all details are correct and consistent. This is extremely important! It's easy to miss errors in simple things like your phone number and employment dates.

✉ **Use good paper.** Use good white or off-white cotton bond paper. The quality of paper to look for would be 20- or 24-pound; 25 percent cotton; or recycled if you like. There are many selections of paper color and style. Resist the wild colors. You need to impress the reader with content, not paper color. You can buy nice resume paper at office supply stores. If you are faxing your resume to employers, plain white paper is fine. You can buy business envelopes to match resume paper stock. If you are applying to a large company that may be scanning resumes, however, mail your resume flat in a 9 x 12-inch envelope. Be sure to add extra postage.

✉ **Make crisp copies.** Laser printing is best; just print resumes from a laser printer as needed. This also allows you to modify your resume as needed for a particular opening. High-quality photocopying of an original is fine also, although you won't be able to target each resume. Copying a copy is not acceptable.

✉ **Avoid writing anything negative.** Simply leave out the underlined material shown in the examples below. On a resume, you don't have to tell the employer everything.

Member, Tennis Team, 1996-1997; <u>resigned due to injury.</u>

Driver, Papa Johns Pizza, 1997-1998. <u>Reason for leaving: speeding tickets.</u>

GPA: <u>1.9/4.0</u>

✉ **Always be honest in your resume**. Do not embellish your resume dishonestly.

✉ **Update your resume regularly**. You should plan on updating your resume at least once a year. Add new courses, workshops, community service positions, honors, activities, and jobs.

- **Allow for white space on your resume.** The usual resume margins are 1 to 1.25 inches all around the resume. Between resume sections, allow 1 or 1.5 returns. Spacing between employer names and job titles can be a full return if space permits. Good use of white space makes a resume easy to read.

A Grammar Lesson for Resume Writing

This section covers the grammar basics of writing a resume. If grammar is not one of your strengths, you should have someone else read your resume for correctness and consistency.

Limited Use of the Personal Pronoun "I"

It's okay to write without a noun or personal pronoun in a resume. In fact, it's better than starting every sentence with "I did this. . . I did that. . ."

For instance, here's the incorrect way to write the duties of a telemarketer position:

- I received inbound telephone calls and answered customers' questions.

- I searched the computer system and gave account information.

- I followed up and mailed corrected statements.

The following sounds much better. The emphasis is on your performance and skills:

- Received inbound telephone calls and answered customers' questions.

- Searched the computer system and gave account information.

- Followed up and mailed corrected statements.

Here's another example. Do not write your job description this way:

Mechanic's Assistant   **January 1998–Present**
I am responsible for cleaning cars and organizing parts. I speak to customers about their car's problems and schedule appointments. I assist the mechanics with routine preventive maintenance.

Instead start each sentence with a verb. The reader knows that you did this work:

Mechanic's Assistant   **January 1998–Present**

- Organize and maintain parts inventory.

- Schedule appointments and provide customer services.

- Perform routine preventive maintenance on automobiles.

Be Consistent with Your Use of Verbs

Present job—use present tense verbs. Start your sentences with present tense verbs if you are currently employed:

Safeway Grocery Stores   May 1997–Current
Retail Merchandiser

- Receive, price, and stock shelves for dry goods.
- Assist with inventory and rotate products.
- Provide customer services and information.

Past jobs—use past tense verbs. Start your sentences with verbs that are consistently in the past tense:

Camp Counselor   Summer 1998

- Counseled and planned daily activities for 15 campers.
- Coordinated more than 10 sports events for campers.
- Coached girls' intramural soccer teams.
- Assisted with kitchen management.

Other Points to Consider

Colons. Using a colon after a resume heading is optional:

EDUCATION: *OR*   EDUCATION

Ampersands. Ampersands are not appropriate in the body text of a resume. You can use them in headings:

Writing & Editing

Grammar errors. Grammar errors can be found by reading the resume in context. The spell checker won't pick up "their" versus "they're," "it's" versus "its," or "your" versus "you're." Consult a grammar book or dictionary as needed.

> **TIP** *It's* is a contraction of *it is*. *Its* is the possessive form of *it*. Example: *It's helpful to describe your job and its duties.*

Putting Your Resume Together

When you write and format your resume information, use a PC or Macintosh and your favorite word processing software. Be sure to save the document on disk frequently as you write.

> ### To Do:
>
> Compile all the information from the worksheets in Chapters 3 and 4 for your resume data file. Then build your first resume (either a college resume or a targeted resume). Refer to examples in this book as needed. What did you learn about yourself as you built your first resume?
>
> _____
>
> _____
>
> _____
>
> _____

> **TIP** Print your resume a few times as you work on the formatting. This will let you see how it looks on paper and let you adjust spacing, alignment, type size, and other elements.

Saving Your Resume on a PC or Macintosh Disk

Here are some pointers for saving your resume electronically, so that you can easily modify and print it when needed.

✉ If you keep your resume on a hard disk, you should back it up on a floppy and keep it somewhere safe. You should also keep a printed copy of the resume for easy reference.

✉ Save your resumes with file names that you can identify easily. You might have three different resume files: resume data, a college resume, and a targeted resume. By giving each file a distinctive name, you will be able to find it without a time-consuming search.

✉ You should also save your basic cover letter, reference list, and thank-you letter electronically. This will make them easy to tailor to each potential employer. Information on writing these last three items appears in the next chapter.

Resume Database File

Your resume database is the long version with everything from your school and work history. The length of this file may be three or four pages. This will be your master information document that you can use to write either a college or targeted resume. You can add information to this file as you gain experience.

To Do:

What is the name of your resume data file? _____

Where is it stored? _____

College Resume File

This file contains your resume for use with college applications. As explained in Chapter 2, the format is a comprehensive overview of education, activities, and employment. It should be one page if possible. Exceptions can be two pages long.

> ### To Do:
>
> What is the name of your college resume file? _____
>
> Where is it stored? _____

Targeted Resume File

This file is for a targeted resume, which features key words and a focused skills section. A targeted resume is usually one-page long.

> ### To Do:
>
> What is the name of your targeted resume file? _____
>
> Where is it stored? _____

Cover Letter File

This file is for your basic cover letter, which is used to introduce your skills and interests to an employer or internship program. You can insert the file's information below after reading Chapter 6.

> ### To Do:
>
> What is the name of your cover letter file? _____
>
> Where is it stored? _____

Reference List File

This file is for your reference list, which you give to potential employers on request. You can insert the file's information next after reading Chapter 6.

> ### *To Do:*
>
> What is the name of your reference list file? _____
>
> Where is it stored? _____

Thank-You Letter File

Keep a thank-you letter on file to use after a personal or telephone interview for a job or internship. You can insert the file's information below after reading Chapter 6.

> ### *To Do:*
>
> What is the name of your thank-you letter file? _____
>
> Where is it stored? _____

The Final Touch

Congratulations—your first resume is done. Depending on your future needs, you may use this resume as is, adjust it for specific jobs, or refer to it to create a completely new resume. For now, you want to make sure this resume is accurate, consistent, and correct.

> ### *To Do:*
>
> Carefully proofread your first resume. Did you notice any errors? List them here, as a reminder to watch for similar errors in future versions. Be sure to correct these errors in your electronic resume file.
>
> _____
>
> _____
>
> Have someone else proofread your resume. List any errors that person finds here. Be sure to correct these errors in your electronic resume file.
>
> _____
>
> _____

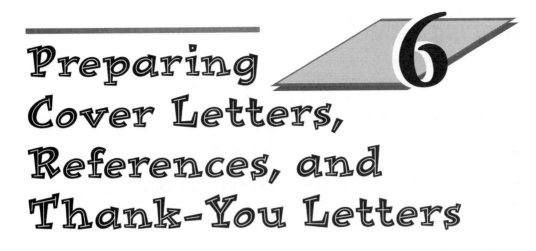

Preparing Cover Letters, References, and Thank-You Letters

"Your reference should outline my good qualities.
Here's a list to get you started."

You need to write cover letters, reference lists, and thank-you letters during your job search. A cover letter accompanies your resume and is a personal introduction and background summary that will impress the reader. Most cover letters have three or four paragraphs. Next, an employer may ask for two to four references who know about your experience and abilities. Be ready with a list of references. This single sheet of paper gives the contact information of those who have agreed to be your references. Finally, the thank-you letter is just that—a short letter saying thank you after an interview. All of these documents are important elements in your job search package.

Creating Great Cover Letters

Without a strong cover letter, your wonderful resume may not get a first glance. The goals of the cover letter are to

✉ Get potential employers interested in you.

✉ Impress them with your experience and skills related to a job opening.

✉ Show your interest in their company and their customers.

✉ Show that you are dependable, professional, and determined.

✉ Make employers want to look at your resume.

The cover letter is as important as your resume. Sample cover letters in this chapter show how to highlight experiences that will interest employers. Do not be bashful about saying that you were a champion swimmer, had a main role in the school play, or are on the school's baseball team. Potential employers will think you are a great student with energy and enthusiasm. They will want you to bring that enthusiasm to their business! Let your cover letter highlight your strong points.

> **TIP** TO CREATE A PROFESSIONAL IMPRESSION, GIVE YOUR COVER LETTER THE SAME LOOK AS YOUR RESUME. USE THE SAME TYPE FONTS AND PAPER STOCK. ALSO, DO NOT STAPLE THE LETTER AND RESUME TOGETHER BECAUSE EMPLOYERS MAY WANT TO PHOTOCOPY YOUR RESUME EASILY. SEND THE LETTER AND RESUME IN A MATCHING ENVELOPE. IF YOU'RE MAILING TO A LARGE COMPANY, SEND THE RESUME AND LETTER FLAT IN A LARGE ENVELOPE IN CASE YOUR RESUME WILL BE SCANNED.

Using a job ad from the *Washington Post,* you now will learn how to write a cover letter. Here's the *Washington Post* ad:

TELEMARKETER. Enjoys speaking with the public. Articulate, computer literate with sales ability. 40 hours, 12 weeks. Send resume to Mr. Paul Jones, Supervisor, Smythe Corp., 1900 M St., NW, Wash., DC 20006. No calls accepted.

Information About You

Start your cover letter with your contact information. Use the same format and type fonts as on your resume:

Kimberly Ann Garrett
2989 Smithwood Avenue
Annapolis, MD 99999
(555) 555-5555

Date

Next list the date, as you would on any business letter:

September 29, 1998

Contact Person's Name, Title, Employer, and Address

Then enter the contact person's name, title, employer, and mailing address. You need to have your letter on a disk so you can personalize and modify it each time. Because it is so easy to use a computer and save your letter, each letter can be individualized quickly. Here is how to set up the person's name and address:

Mr. Paul Jones
Supervisor
Smythe Corp.
1900 M Street, NW
Washington, DC 20006

But what if you are applying for an advertised job that does not give an individual's name? Then try to find the name of the hiring person or the person reviewing incoming resumes. Put some effort into searching for a name. Using a name can get your letter and resume to the hiring manager more quickly and can be an effective personal touch.

If you know which department has the opening, you can call the company and ask the operator for the department manager's name. You can also search the company's Web site and try to find the manager's name. If you're applying to a giant corporation and the ad says "Human Resources Director, Marriott Corporation," expect that your resume will be scanned. In this last case, you may not be able to get an individual's name.

Salutation

Here are your choices for addressing the contact person:

Dear Mr. Jones:	If a man's name is the contact.
Dear Ms. Smith:	If a woman's name is the contact.
Dear Prospective Employer:	If there is no name.

Opening Paragraph

Here are four types of opening paragraphs, depending on how you learned of the position:

Classified Advertisement

> I read your advertisement in the Washington Post for a Telemarketer on Sept. 28, 1998.

Unsolicited Mailing

With an unsolicited mailing, you send companies your resume without being asked or without seeing a specific ad, just in case they need someone like you. Unsolicited resumes are usually not effective, so try to talk with managers at companies you're interested in before sending resumes.

> I would like to apply for a position as a Telemarketer with Smythe Corporation. I am seeking a summer position where I can use my communications skills and work with the public.

The Internet

You may also find leads on Internet job sites and company Web sites. Here is how to write an opening paragraph for such a lead:

> I am sending my enclosed resume as an application for the Telemarketer position with your company. I found the opening listed on your Web site. Based on the description of Smythe Corporation, I would like to work for a company like yours. I am seeking a position where I can use my communications skills and work with the public.

Referral

A *referral* is a job lead from a neighbor, friend, mentor, or someone else in your network. Sometimes a person in your network will speak to the hiring person about you. This is truly the best way to find a job. Employers appreciate referrals. Referrals save them from reviewing hundreds of applications. Employers trust the recommendation of a valued employee or friend who stated that you would be a good employee. Sometimes departments are filled with the friends of a few people. Referrals are the greatest!

> **TIP** To get referrals, talk to people in your network. Tell them what you're looking for, where, when, and why. They need to know your objectives very well. Ask them to think about leads they might have. Tell them that you will call back in a couple of days. This is an accepted practice for job searches, and you may be amazed at how many job leads you get.

Here are three sample opening paragraphs for a cover letter based on a referral:

Sample 1. I am sending my resume to you because of a referral from Mike Thomas, an associate in your Annapolis store. I am seeking a summer internship where I can use my communications skills and work with the public.

Sample 2. I was referred to you by Mike Thomas, who is my neighbor. He tells me that you frequently hire dependable, hard-working high school seniors in your telemarketing department.

Sample 3. I was referred to you by Mike Thomas, who is a member of my church and a longtime family friend. I understand you are hiring student interns in your telemarketing department. Mike recommended that I write to you and send my resume for your consideration.

Middle Paragraph

Next is a summary of your background and critical skills (hard skills) to show you are a match for the position:

> As my resume indicates, I am active in theater in high school and had excellent roles in two plays. I am also successful in debate and student government. With these experiences, I can offer you excellent communication and interpersonal skills. I maintain a 3.0 average and worked 10 hours per week during the school year. Familiarity with PCs, Windows 95, Word 7.0, and Microsoft Office Suite is another skill I can bring to your department. I use the Internet regularly and can keyboard more than 45 words per minute.

Second Middle Paragraph

This is your persuasive paragraph with a few soft skills.

> If you are seeking a dependable, hard-working, and friendly young person to work in your department for the summer, I would like to be considered.

Creating a Lead List

When you get referrals for job openings, use the following format to keep track of leads. You can use a 3 x 5 card for each lead or keep entries on your computer.

Referral person:
Mike Thomas

Name of lead: Paul Jones

Title: Supervisor, Telemarketing Department

Company: Smythe Corp.

Address:
1900 M Street, NW, Washington, DC 20006

Telephone: (555) 555-8888

Fax: (555) 555-9999

E-mail address:
pjones@smythe.com

How my referral knows this person:
Racquetball partner

Job opening: Possible summer internship in telemarketing department.

Follow up: Mike will speak to Mr. Jones about me by Friday. I am to send Mr. Jones a resume.

Contact Information and Closing

I am available afternoons at (555) 555-5555 after 4 p.m. I have voicemail on that number. I will call you in a couple of days to see if I can make an appointment to discuss a summer position. Thank you for your time and consideration.

Sincerely,

Kimberly Ann Garrett

Kimberly Ann Garrett

Enclosure: resume

If your resume and letter were sent in response to a classified ad with no phone number, or if the company is large and receiving hundreds of resumes, you may not be able to call. In that case, state "I look forward to hearing from you soon."

> **TIP** THINK ABOUT THE COMPANY'S PRODUCTS AND SERVICES WHEN YOU WRITE YOUR COVER LETTER. THINK ABOUT THE HIRING PERSON'S NEEDS. HOW COULD YOU HELP THIS PERSON WITH HIS OR HER DEPARTMENT? WOULD YOU BE GOOD WITH THE COMPANY'S CUSTOMERS? IF SO, THE COMPANY WOULD BE LUCKY TO HAVE YOU, RIGHT? GET THE MANAGER TO RECOGNIZE YOUR INTEREST AND TALENTS THROUGH YOUR LETTER AND RESUME.

Cover Letter Samples

The following student is responding to an ad for a part-time position in computer repair. The letter highlights his computer skills and experience. The bullet style is easy to read and write because each entry is a statement, not a full sentence. The paragraph style is written with full sentences. Which one do you prefer?

Here is the ad, followed by the student's letter:

> **Help Wanted: Computer Technician.** Hardware and software experience. Must have Windows 3.0 and 95 conversion experience. Ability to communicate with nontechnical users. One year experience required. 20 hours/week. Send resume and letter to Andy E. Quinn, ABC Computers, 322 Smith Street, Lockport, NY 20000. No phone calls.

Garth Torres
618 Willingham Road
Lockport, NY 20000
(555) 555-3333
E-mail: gtorres@com.com

May 18, 1998

Mr. Andy E. Quinn
ABC Computers
322 Smith Street
Lockport, NY 20000

Dear Mr. Quinn:

I am responding to your advertisement in the *Gaithersburg Gazette* for a Computer Technician in your computer repair business.

Block paragraph style

As a Junior at Little Valley Central High School in Little Valley, New York, I have completed numerous computer courses, including Microsoft Suite and PC Maintenance. I have upgraded the hardware and software of my own PC over the last three years. I also successfully upgraded my system and friends' PCs from Windows 3.0 to Windows 95. As an assistant in the school's computer lab, I currently help students with various computer needs. I am a student support person for the school office as well.

Bullet style

I can offer your computer firm the following qualifications:

♦ Junior at Little Valley Central High School, Little Valley, New York, with 20 hours per week available.

♦ Completed five courses in computers, including Microsoft Suite, PC Maintenance, and Windows 95.

♦ Owned and operated PCs for three years.

♦ Installed software, including Windows 3.0 to Windows 95; upgraded memory and hardware.

♦ Assistant in computer lab and school office for eight months; help with 15 PCs.

I would like to work part-time throughout my senior year in high school to gain professional experience in computer repair, troubleshooting, and installation. With my computer background and ability to communicate with users, I would be a good addition to your company. I am available for an interview at your convenience. Thank you for your time.

Sincerely,

Garth Torres

Garth Torres

Enclosure: Resume

The next letter was sent by a student because of a referral. The student knows about the company, its work ethic, and the testing process for job applicants because her neighbor, John Carruthers, explained it to her. AE&E is a public utility that hires people who have some technical capability (the company gives a test for this), who have been dependable throughout school (decent grades, and so on), and who will take good care of their customers.

Jennifer Dean
3456 Rogers Ford Avenue
Hanover, PA 22222

December 3, 1998

Ms. Jane Howard
Supervisor, Installation Department
AE&E
344 Center Street
Baltimore, MD 22222

Dear Ms. Howard:

I was referred to you by my neighbor, John Carruthers, who told me about your department and services. I will be graduating from Milford Mill Senior High School in May and would like to be considered for your training program.

I will have completed a general course of study in school, and I am skilled in using PCs with Word and WordPerfect. My work history includes two summers in new home and rehab construction. I have good references from supervisors and coworkers regarding my ability to work hard and my skill level. I am able to use power tools and can work very well with a construction crew.

John has told me about the emphasis that AE&E places on customer service. I have gained good communications skills as a Big Sister mentor for a 10-year-old-girl. I have spoken to her teachers and parents about her studies and progress, and they appreciate my time with her.

I am available to meet with you and complete your tests and other processes at your request. If you need further information, please contact me after 3 p.m. daily at (555) 555-7777. Thank you for your time and consideration. I look forward to your response.

Sincerely,

Jennifer Dean

Jennifer Dean

Enclosure: resume

To Do:

In a newspaper or on the Internet, look for two interesting ads for part-time or summer work. What experience, hard skills, and soft skills would you stress in the cover letter for each job?

Ad 1 job title: _____

What I would stress in a cover letter: _____

_____

_____

Ad 2 job title: _____

What I would stress in a cover letter: _____

_____

_____

References—An Important Part of the Job Application Package

References are people who know the quality of your work. They are usually former supervisors, teachers, coaches, ministers, longtime family friends, and counselors. To use a person as a reference, you need to ask that person if you can put him or her on your reference list with a telephone number. It's good if you can list from two to five references.

After a personal or phone interview, the employer may call a reference and ask questions. Some questions might be

✉ How long have you known this student?

✉ What type of work did the student do for you?

✉ What are the student's strongest and weakest skills?

✉ Did the student arrive at school or work on time?

✉ Would you hire the student again?

As you can see from the questions, references are very important. You need to develop and keep track of people who will be your references. You should tell references what you're looking for so that they will be responsive to a potential employer who calls.

> **TIP** YOU CAN ALSO REQUEST LETTERS OF RECOMMENDATION FROM YOUR REFERENCES. THIS IS HELPFUL IF YOU SEND OUT NUMEROUS RESUMES OR NEED LETTERS FOR COLLEGE APPLICATIONS.

This is what a good reference list will look like. Because you will give this to a potential employer, it should match your resume's look.

Kenny T. Day
1010 Edmondson Avenue
Louisville, KY 22222
(555) 444-4444

References

Janice J. Benjamin, President
New Options, Inc.
2311 E. Stadium, Suite B-2
Mount Washington, KY 22222
(555) 555-0000—Work
Supervisor, Internship, New Options, Summer 1997

Jane Sommer, Director
Sports Management Department
Smith College
84 Elm Street
Frankfort, KY 22222
(555) 555-0000
Swimming Coach, 5 years

Judith Dowd
Paris Country School
Paris, KY 33333
(555) 555-8888–School
(555) 555-9999–Home
Instructor for Art History, Archaeology, and Student Advisor

Lester Minsuk, CPA
29 Exeter Road
Bardstown, KY 33333
(555) 555-3333—Work
(555) 555-4444—Home
Family Friend and Mentor for career in Finance

You can give your reference list to your potential employer three ways:

✉ Send it with your resume initially if requested.

✉ Bring it with you to the interview.

✉ Send it after an interview when the employer is seriously considering you for hire.

To Do:

You listed three possible references in Chapter 1. Call these people and ask if they would serve as your references. Get complete, accurate contact information for each person. Start your reference list here. Then format your reference list on a computer and save it electronically. Print out a copy and proofread it carefully.

Reference 1 name: _____

Title: _____

Company name and address: _____

_____

Phone numbers: _____

My relationship with this person: _____

Reference 2 name: _____

Title: _____

Company name and address: _____

_____

Phone numbers: _____

My relationship with this person: _____

Reference 3 name: _____

Title: _____

Company name and address: _____

_____

Phone numbers: _____

My relationship with this person: _____

Writing Thank-You Letters

After an interview or meeting with a potential employer, mentor, or individual who may give you an internship, send a thank-you letter. This is a great opportunity to bring your name up to that person again and express interest in the position. The thank-you letter reminds this person that you are a candidate and shows that you are very considerate, interested, and appreciative.

The thank-you letter is where you once more thank the person for his or her time and for giving you information about the job and the company. You can also compliment the employer on the organization's plans, programs, and anything else that impressed you. This letter needs to be genuine. Don't make a general statement like, "I thought your business looked great." You need to say something like, "I was impressed with how professional everyone was and how customers were well taken care of by your employees."

Employers like to know that you noticed their business, employees, and customers. When you're in an interview, pay attention to your surroundings. Check out the displays, signs, windows, and inventory. If you like what you see, then you can say that in your thank-you letter.

If your thank-you letter is very short, you could hand-write this note. You could buy a conservative note card at a stationery store and write: "Thank you very much for your time on Monday. I am very interested in your hotel management training program. I look forward to hearing from you soon."

Here is a more formal thank-you letter. The type fonts and paper stock should match your resume.

Laura C. Barrett
10309 Arlington Boulevard
Des Plaines, IL 99999
(555) 555-9999
lbarrett@net.net

July 5, 1998

Ms. Carol Waters
Manager
Perfect Touch Hair Salon
312 Frederick Road
Suite 782
Des Plaines, IL 99999

Dear Ms. Waters:

I enjoyed our interview today and the tour you gave me of your salon. Your new expanded salon is beautiful and efficient, and it looks as if it will be very successful.

As I said in the interview, I would like to be a retail sales associate for your products. I like cosmetics and fashion products, and it would be a pleasure to talk about and sell what I so enjoy. Additionally, I believe that I could help you with marketing to high school students.

Thank you again for your time. I look forward to hearing from you about the position.

Sincerely,

Laura C. Barrett

Laura C. Barrett

TIP WRITE AND MAIL YOUR THANK-YOU LETTER WITHIN 24 HOURS OF AN INTERVIEW, WHEN IT IS STILL FRESH IN YOUR MIND AND THE EMPLOYER'S MIND.

To Do:

For one of the ads you found earlier, imagine that you have interviewed for the position. Write a thank-you note for your interview.

_____

_____

_____

_____

_____

_____

_____

_____

_____

_____

_____

_____

_____

_____

_____

_____

_____

_____

_____

_____

_____

Student Resume Case Studies

"Actually, we transform into superheroes by polishing our resumes."

In this chapter, you will meet more students who share their backgrounds, aspirations, and resumes. These students have accomplished something in their high school years—good grades, involvement in sports and clubs, special awards, volunteer work, and paid jobs. Some of the students are involved in many different activities. Other students focus on one or two areas. A few of these students have definite ideas about their futures. Others aren't sure. Their resumes reflect what they've done, what they're interested in, and what they hope to become.

Whether a sophomore, junior, or senior, none of these students is a donothing. They got involved in what interests them, are trying different things, and are ready for the chance to grow and learn. These examples show that it's not too early for you to start gaining experiences that will be a lot of fun now and serve you well in the future.

> **TIP** NOTE THAT MOST OF THESE STUDENTS ARE THINKING ABOUT THEIR FUTURE EDUCATIONS ALONG WITH THEIR FUTURE CAREERS. TO RESEARCH THE EDUCATION AND TRAINING NEEDED FOR SPECIFIC JOBS, CONSULT RESOURCES LIKE THE *OCCUPATIONAL OUTLOOK HANDBOOK*.

Sophomore Will Experiment with Science Career

Russell Fenton

Russell Fenton says, "I really like school, especially science and sports. Right now I would like to continue my studies in the sciences and stay physically active. I hope to get a summer internship at a science laboratory to gain some science-related work experience."

He adds, "As a member of the Young Astronauts Club, I learned about study programs in the sciences and am familiar with the qualifications required to pursue a science career. I'm going in that direction, but we'll see what happens when I get to college."

Russ is involved in many activities and gaining many experiences. In an exception to usual practice, Russ's resume includes some activities and awards from before high school because they are science-related. As Russ gains more experience, he will drop these early achievements from his resume.

RUSSELL FENTON

29 Midspring Lane / Rutland, VT 55555 / (555) 555-8888

GOAL

To gain experience in the field of science as a summer intern at a science laboratory

EDUCATION

Rutland Country School Upper School, Rutland, VT, 1996–present

Academic   Maintained honor roll status for two consecutive years
Won eighth grade science prize and science fair awards

Clubs   Member, Math Club, 1996-present
Member, Young Astronauts Club, 1992–1996

> Science-related experience

Sports   Rutland Country School Tennis, Spring 1998
Rutland Country School Basketball, 1997-1998
Rutland Country School Soccer, Fall 1997

Special Abilities/Recognition
Star rank in the Boy Scouts of America with 19 merit badges, 1995–present
Working toward Eagle Scout badge
Computer skills: Proficient in the use of PCs and Macs

EMPLOYMENT

Child care for children ages 3-10, Summer 1998
Contact: Mrs. Gwen Moore, (555) 555-0000

Summer School Assistant at Rutland Country School, Summer 1997
Contact: Mrs. June McFadden, (555) 999-9999

VOLUNTEER ACTIVITIES

National Aquarium in Baltimore–Student Exhibit Guide, Summer 1997
Our Daily Bread Soup Kitchen in Rutland, VT, Summer 1996

PERSONAL

Certified in Basic First Aid and CPR
Hobbies: Model building (all types) and stamp collecting

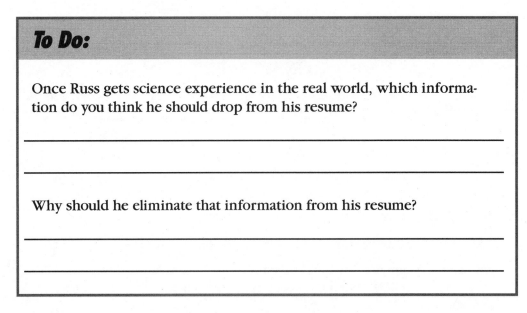

To Do:

Once Russ gets science experience in the real world, which information do you think he should drop from his resume?

_____

_____

Why should he eliminate that information from his resume?

_____

_____

Sophomore Shoots for TV Broadcasting Career

Stephanie Gage

Stephanie Gage says, "My career goal is to become an anchor for a major television station. I would like to enter a college that has one of the best mass media programs available. My hope is that excellent grades will land me a television broadcasting internship."

She goes on to say, "I understand that this field is a hard one to conquer and extremely competitive. But I know I can handle anything as long as I am prepared." Stephanie's strong grades, excellent communications skills, and outgoing personality are sure to help her attain her goal.

STEPHANIE GAGE
455 Montrose Avenue
Cincinnati, OH 22222
(555) 555-5555

EDUCATION

WASHINGTON HIGH SCHOOL, Cincinnati, OH
Graduation expected June 2000

Academic Honors
Honor Roll, average 3.5/4.0
Gifted and Talented English coursework, 1997-present

Activities
Yearbook Staff, WHS, 1997-present
- Take photos at school events
- Write captions
- Proofread

Reporter, *The Patriot,* WHS newspaper, 1997-present
- Write news and feature stories
- Proofread
- Assist with layout

> Communications-related background

WORK EXPERIENCE

Responsible for the safety and care of children for the following families:

Mr. and Mrs. C. Gillis (daughter age 2), Loveland, OH, 1997-present
Dr. and Mrs. J. Vasquez (twin boys age 2), Cincinnati, OH, 1996

COMPUTER SKILLS

PC: Windows 95, WordPerfect
Macintosh: Microsoft Works

VOLUNTEER SERVICE

Mentor—Assisted teachers and staff with instructional activities to increase eighth grade students' aptitude in mathematics and science, Summer 1997

Sophomore Has Designs on Fashion Industry or Event Planning

Lauren Trenton

Lauren Trenton says, "If I relate what I like to do now to what I might want to do for a career, I'd say that I like to give parties and to shop!" On a more serious note, Lauren says, "The events at school and home that I have been involved in planning are always successful, and everybody says I have a good eye for fashion." Lauren is considering both the fashion industry, possibly as a retail buyer for a major department store, or a special events coordinator position for a corporation.

"I'm going to major in business and pursue internships in areas of interest to me. I want to go to a college where cooperative learning is emphasized so I can gain experience. It is important to me to enjoy what I do for a living."

• **Lauren Marie Trenton** •
101 Edmondson Avenue
Springfield, IL 66666
(555) 555-3333
e-mail: ltrenton@ari.net

Education

Springfield High School, Springfield, IL
Sophomore; expect to graduate May 2000
Honor Roll, 1997-1998

Activities

Sophomore Class Vice-President—School Year 1997-1998
   Lead meetings, plan events, plan fundraising.

Member of Future Business Leaders of America—School Year 1997-1998

Freshman Class Treasurer—School Year 1996-1997
   Handle budgets, fundraising, and cash control.

> Varied experiences in both event planning and fashion

Employment

The Perfect Touch Springfield, IL (15 hours/week)—July-October 1997
Retail Sales and Cosmetics Consultant for Merle Norman Cosmetics
   Assisted with product merchandising, inventory control, displays, and customer service.

Sam's Bagels, Springfield, IL (15 hours/week)—March-June 1997
   Prepared sandwiches and operated cash register.

Specialized Training

Two-month internship with training for Merle Norman Cosmetics—1997

Skills Summary

Leadership and organizational skills
Customer service and public relations skills
PC and Macintosh with Windows 95 and Word 6
Internet and e-mail

> Skills Summary can move to the top and be more focused once she has a clear goal in mind

To Do:

Which activities to date would help Lauren with a fashion career?

_____

_____

Which activities to date would help Lauren with an event-planning career?

_____

_____

Junior Has Many Interests but Uncertain Objectives

Kylie Jennings

Kylie Jennings says, "I am going to major in philosophy in college. I am not clear about what job I will get after college, but I am certain that it will all work out."

Kylie is content to be uncertain of her career objectives at this time. She has confidence that her degree and skills will lead her in the right direction. Her skills are obvious: foreign languages, math, business, and science. By the time she completes college, a career in one of these areas will become obvious.

Kylie Marie Jennings

124 Hana Avenue/Haiku, HI/(555) 555-9999/email: KYLIE@ARI.NET

EDUCATION	**Hall College Preparatory,** Olinda, Maui, Hawaii
	Expect to graduate in 1999
	Academic Courses
	Headmaster's List, GPA: 3.9 (1997-1998 school year)
	Japanese I and Spanish IV
	Honors Physics, Pre-Calculus, and Spanish
	Activities
	Member, Cross-Country and Track Teams
	Second in Maui County, 1996
WORKSHOPS	Smyth School of Art, Washington, DC, Summer 1997—Studio Art and Photography
	Costa Rica, South America, Summer 1996—Spanish Language Immersion
EMPLOYMENT	**Maui Retail Corp.,** Lahaina, Maui, 1996 to present
	Retail Sales/Computer Assistant to the Regional Manager

- Perform computer research concerning inventory, costs, and store information
- Research competitive companies, products, and catalogs via the Internet
- Manipulate online data to create sales and financial reports
- Develop formulas and create Excel spreadsheets, graphs, and reports for management and financial analysis by managers
- Retail sales, customer service, inventory control, and merchandising

> Numerous areas of strength are obvious

SKILLS	*Languages: Fluent Spanish; currently studying Japanese*
	Computers: PCs with Windows 95, Excel, Word 6.0, Internet, e-mail
INTERESTS	Extensive travel in the U.S. and South America
	Hawaiian culture and history
	Philosophy and environmental sciences
	Outdoor activities, including hiking, camping, and biking
PERSONAL QUALITIES	Dependable, hard-working, motivated, sincere, and analytical
	Challenged by learning and new experiences

> Soft skills

To Do:

Based on her background so far, in which area does Kylie seem to have the most experience?

_____

_____

_____

How do you know that Kylie will be successful in whatever she chooses for a career?

_____

_____

_____

Senior Follows Path for Outdoor Work

Terry Richards

You met Terry Richards through his resumes earlier in the book. Terry's resumes appear in Chapter 5 as formatting examples. Terry is using those resumes to apply for retail jobs at recreation equipment stores during his junior year. The resume here shows a new objective: a summer internship with the Natural Resources Conservation Corps (part of the U.S. Department of Agriculture).

TERRY R. RICHARDS

25 Esposito Lane
Bakersfield, California 90000
(555) 555-5555

Objective

Field Intern—Natural Resources Conservation Corps

Skills & Knowledge

- Knowledge and experience in outdoor recreation and parks.
- Firsthand experience with trail construction tools and equipment.
- Communication and instruction skills in use of equipment, tools, and methods.
- Experienced in crew living and camping in the backcountry for a total of 20 months.
- Knowledge of environmental programs and importance of minimum impact camping.

Work Experience

CALIFORNIA CONSERVATION CORPS

CORPS MEMBER/TRAIL WORKER (paid position)   Summer 1998

KLAMATH NATIONAL FOREST, SHASTA TRINITY NATIONAL FOREST, KINGS CANYON NATIONAL PARK

- Maintained trails, constructed rock work, and rehabilitated damaged meadows.
- Constructed causeway, single and multitier rockwall, inside and outside drains and wash pans over slickrock and through trail sections that have undergone erosion and water damage.
- Camp life: Lived and worked with 18 people in the crew for four months in the backcountry. Shared kitchen patrol duties; relocated camp frequently; hiked trail and cross-country tours for as far as 20 miles round-trip; attended four classes per week in related subjects.
- Equipment: Crosscuts (saw), picks, pulawskis, sledge hammers, chinking hammers, shovels, loppers, pinonjars, dirt buckets, blasting equipment.

SALMON RESTORATION SPECIALIST (paid position)   April 1997—April 1998

SALMON RESTORATION PROJECTS/FISHERIES AND OIL RECYCLING EDUCATION

- Constructed salmon restoration sites.
- Utilized natural materials to improve the salmon habitat.
- Repaired damaged sections of riparian zones.

> Completely targeted to outdoor work

Special Skills & Awards

- Presentations concerning environmental effects of oil recycling, 1998.
- Corps Member of the Month, March 1998.

Education & Training

Bakersfield High School, Bakersfield, California—Expect to graduate May 1999.

Other Training: How to Pack for the Backcountry, 3/98, 20 hours; Minimum Impact Camping, 4/98, 20 hours; Basic First Aid, 5/98, 10 hours; River Rescue, 6/98, 8 hours.

Other Interests

Member of soccer team (goalkeeper). Also enjoy basketball, mountain biking, photography (35mm), in addition to camping and hiking.

Terry Richards says, "For me, high school is a means to an end. Luckily, I've had some good jobs that held my interest. I love trail work—building paths and improving properties for hikers. I hope to eventually get an apprenticeship that will lead to a career in landscape architecture."

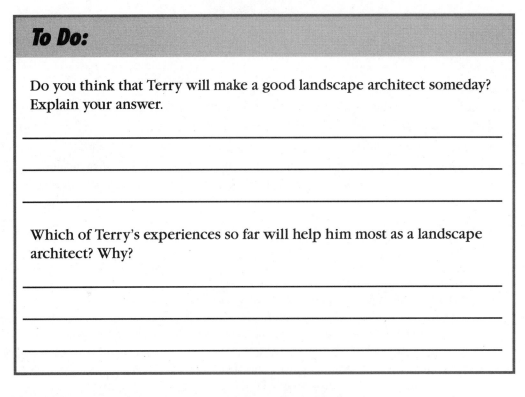

To Do:

Do you think that Terry will make a good landscape architect someday? Explain your answer.

_____

_____

_____

Which of Terry's experiences so far will help him most as a landscape architect? Why?

_____

_____

_____

Senior Composes Music Career

Michael Hill

Michael Hill says, "I know that I'll be working with music, either as a recording engineer, digital composer, sound system designer, music teacher, or maybe with kids in music therapy. First, I plan to complete my 1st Engineer's License to gain a certificate in recording and engineering. Then I'll work toward my B.S. degree in music theory, composition, or whatever music emphasis I decide later on. I look forward to more internships and work in my field."

Michael Hill
555 Pine Lane • San Antonio, TX 21228
Home: (555) 555-9999 • Work: (555) 555-2222
E-mail: chill@com.com

EDUCATION

Carver School for the Performing Arts, San Antonio, TX
Graduated 1998
Major courses

Music Theory I and II	Piano Performance (all 4 years)
Audio Production	Composition
Sound Engineering	Digital Music

Focuses
entirely on a
music career

Evans College, Donna, TX, Summer, 1997
Electronic and computer music workshops.
Manders Institute, Houston, TX, 1990-1994
Private piano study.

INTERNSHIP

Alpha School of Applied Recording Arts and Sciences, San Antonio, TX, 12-week program, Summer 1997
Alpha is a major multistudio complex with four professional recording studios. Internship in recording and engineering under acoustician John Garmer. Assisted engineering for KHFS program "Just Passing Through."

SKILLS

Digital and acoustic music composition and arrangement.
Recording and engineering.
Sound system installation in homes and automobiles.
Excellent communications skills.

ELECTRONIC MUSIC EQUIPMENT

Home Studio with PC: Digital Sampler ASR 10, Denon 3-head, 2-track tape deck, NAD 1600 preamp, Nakamichi STASIS amp, Infinity Ref, Series II; PC with Cakewalk, Mackie 24x8, Alesis Adat; Tascam DAT MK30II.
Car Stereo: Sony Disc player, Carver 4650 amp, MTX active crossover, Boston Acoustic 4.0's, Celestion 12" 4 ohm.
Performance: keyboard, electric bass, various acoustic instruments.

EMPLOYMENT

Washington Music Center, San Antonio, TX, 1996-1998
Keyboard sales and warehouse work.
Entertaining Interiors, San Antonio, TX 1995
Residential home theater installation.

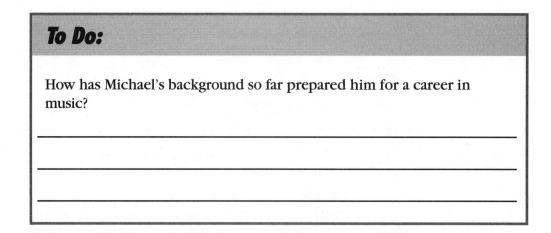

To Do:

How has Michael's background so far prepared him for a career in music?

_____

_____

_____

Sky's the Limit for Graduate Who Thought He'd Be an Astronomer

Chris Rogers

Chris Rogers enjoyed science in high school and is now a successful Web publisher. Chris is sharing parts of his high school resume and current resume so that you can see how much he has accomplished between the ages of 18 and 26. Since high school, Chris has tested parts for satellites, established a Web site publishing business, and created the incredibly popular www.gargoyles-fan.org Web site. He hosts the www.highschoolresumes. com Web site, where you can see other high school resumes and job sites.

Chris's comments about high school and careers: "As a high school student, I wanted to pursue astronomy. Then I got my B.A. in Astrophysics and realized that I didn't want to pursue my hobby as a career. But I learned a lot from these experiences and am glad that I did it. Everyone has to find a niche. Today I am very happy with what I'm doing."

Age 18—Student

EDUCATION

Smithburg High School, Smithburg, MD—Graduated 1989

Academics:	AP Physics and Calculus; GPA: 3.8; 4th out of 182
Science Fair Project:	Designed a solar power home with a windmill producing power and solar panels heating the water. Won Energy Conservation Award, Texaco Corporation.
Scholarship:	Buzzy Whitmer Memorial Scholarship—Community Benefactor
Honors:	National Honor Society; Eagle Scout
	Bausch & Lomb Science Award, Honors for Science

EMPLOYMENT HISTORY

Long Meadows Cinemas, Hagerstown, MD, promoted to Assistant Manager, 1987–1991

COMPUTER SKILLS

Macintosh Apple II

Age 26–Successful Web Publisher

EDUCATION

B.A. (Astrophysics) May 1993, University of Virginia

A.A. (Physics) May 1991, Hagerstown Junior College

FIELDS OF SPECIALIZATION

HTML/CGI, Internet/WWW, System Administration Computer/Network Systems, Astronomy/Physics Instrumentation, Optics, Space Hardware Integration and Testing

PROFESSIONAL EXPERIENCE

Wyvern Web Works, Silver Spring, MD   5/96-Present
   Owner, Web Publisher
- Wyvern Web Works (http://www.wyvernweb.com/)
- Gargoyles Fan Website (http://www.gargoyles-fans.org/)—5 million hits/month.

Global Commerce and Information, Columbia, MD   1/98-Present
   Senior Staff Consultant

Hughes Information Technology Systems, Landover, MD   12/96-1/98
   Assistant Web Site Manager/Web Development Engineer

This entire resume (and lots more) is available at www.wyvernweb.com/crogers/resume.html.

To Do:

What do you learn about career planning by studying Chris Rogers's resume segments?

_____

_____

_____

_____

_____

_____

_____

_____

_____

_____

_____

*The resumes of these new high school graduates
will look a lot different in just a few years.*

Job Search Tips

"My distinguished career began fifty years ago when I fired up the old Yahoo search engine and punched in the word *rutabaga*."

The school year will be over soon, and you're thinking about a summer job. Or, a new school year is starting, and you could use a part-time job. In addition to earning money, you want to gain work experience. So you're probably saying, "What kind of job should I look for? How can I find one? Where do I look for a job?" This chapter helps you answer these questions and provides interview tips.

Thinking About the Possibilities

What kind of job should you seek? Consider what interests you have now and what you most enjoy. Is there a potential job in that area of interest? If you have several interests, try for a job in a field related to one of them. By working in one field for the summer or on a part-time basis, you may decide that a certain type of work is not for you. If you're still stuck about what kind of work to pursue, your counselor or career center at school has vocational interest and skill tests that can show where your strengths and career interests lie. *You should take these tests.* They give you great ideas about careers and your abilities. Also check the library for career-related reference books that describe various occupations. Then pursue jobs that fit your interests, abilities, and personality.

Here are some ideas on the types of jobs you could search for based on your current interests:

- **Early childhood education.** If you like kids and have incredible patience, then a position at a day care center, camp, or pool would be good for your resume and your career. Check with your local parks department and YMCA.

- **Law enforcement.** If you aspire to work in law enforcement, then a position in the parks, volunteer fire department, a law firm, bonding agency, or courts would be a great place to work.

- **Finance and business.** If you think you would like to work in business somehow, then search for a position in a business, especially where you can work with numbers, spreadsheets, and reports.

- **Sales.** If you are a natural salesperson (good speaker and outgoing) and think it's possible that you might sell a product that you believe in, try a position in sales. You could do retail sales, route (newspaper) sales, or any other kind of sales. Just get sales experience!

- **Medical.** This includes nursing, physical therapy, occupational therapy, and emergency medicine. If you are interested in medicine, work at a hospital, clinic, physician's office, or EMT service.

- **Veterinary.** If you like animals, then work at an animal hospital, farm, race track, pet store, grooming shop, or for a pet-sitter.

- **Art.** If you like to draw, paint, or use computer graphics programs, look for work at an art museum, newspaper layout department, print shop, or graphic design firm.

- **Plants and gardening.** Do you have a green thumb and enjoy working with plants? Try a job with a landscaping firm, greenhouse, flower shop, gardening center, or tree farm.

- **Computers.** Do people turn to you with their computer questions? Look for work at an Internet service provider, in a computer store, or in a company's technical support department.

To Do:

What kind of work would you like to do for your first or next job? Why?

_____

_____

_____

Getting Leads from Your Network, Mentors, and Parents

Leads are the number one way to find a job. Contact the people in your network (neighbors, former bosses, teachers, counselors, coaches, friends' parents), call your mentor, and talk to your parents. Tell them you're searching for a summer or part-time position, ideally in a certain field (tell them what you would really like to do).

Ask if they have any ideas where you could apply. If they can't think of anything right then, ask if you can call back in a few days to see if they've thought of any referrals. Most people will be willing to help you.

To Do:

List the people in your network. Refer to this list when you are looking for job leads.

Name: _____

Job title: _____

Employer: _____

Phone number: _____

Name: _____

Job title: _____

Employer: _____

Phone number: _____

Name: _____

Job title: _____

Employer: _____

Phone number: _____

Name: _____

Job title: _____

Employer: _____

Phone number: _____

Handling Job Leads

When a job lead comes your way, get as much information as possible about the referred business or person. Here are two pointers on handling job leads:

- ✉ Take detailed notes about the potential employer: company name, telephone number, address, and any insight about the company that your contact may have.

- ✉ Ask your contact how you should approach the person (by phone, fax, or mail). If it's by phone, ask if there is a good time to call. Ask if you can use your contact's name when introducing yourself. It's great if you can mention someone's name as an introduction. If you need to approach a referral by fax or mail, write a cover letter that mentions your contact's name at the beginning. (See Chapter 6.)

Developing a Telephone Script to Contact a Job Lead

When you contact a referred person, you will most likely get his or her attention and probably a few minutes of time because of the relationship the person has with your contact. When calling a referral, be clear, upbeat, confident, and friendly. Be respectful of a referral's time. Ask if the person has a few minutes to talk. If the person is busy, ask when you can call back. Talk somewhat slowly. *Remember that you are selling yourself!*

You could practice your telephone call on videotape or with a friend first. Here's a sample script:

Student: Hi, my name is Kathy Weinstein. I was referred to you by my family's accountant, James Waters. I am a junior at Quincy High and will be majoring in business. I was wondering if I could send you my resume for consideration for any summer work you might have? I have good computer and administrative skills.

Potential employer: Sure, that would be fine. We usually hire one or two clerks for the summer. I'll think about it. Send your resume to me at 555 Main Street.

Student: Thank you. Is it okay if I call you in a week to set up a meeting where we could discuss a summer position? I'm trying to line something up early.

Potential employer: Okay, I'll be talking with you in a few days. Thanks for calling.

Student: Thanks for your time. I'll put my resume in the mail today.

If the person is not interested in hiring summer help, you could ask if the company hires part-time workers during the school year. If the company is not hiring or is not interested, then be polite, thank the person for his or her time, and say that you might contact the company again when you are in college. Write a thank-you note even if the answer is "no." You never know when you will come across the person again.

Following a Lead

Emily's internship with the Department of Interior in Maui came through a lead. Emily's mother visited a friend in Maui who had a friend who was the chief law enforcement officer at Haleakala National Park. Emily and her mom wondered if Haleakala used interns to help with interpretation.

After obtaining the officer's name and number from her mom's friend, Emily called the officer. She asked who was in charge of volunteers and interns. The officer said that the park used interns and gave Emily the instructions to apply. Emily sent her resume. Within four to five months, she was accepted as an intern and went to Maui for three exciting months to live and work.

CASE STUDY

Searching Classified Ads

The best jobs are usually not found in the classifieds. Most jobs are found through friends and leads. But you still should read the classified ads. Occasionally, you will find an interesting job advertisement or company. When you're ready to find a job, follow these steps for reading the classifieds:

1. Buy the Sunday newspaper. Find a space with lots of light (the ads are so small). Get something to drink and eat, since this might take an hour or more.

2. Find scissors, tape or paste, a pen, and a blank 8½ x 11-inch sheet before you start reading the ads.

3. Cut out ads that look interesting and attach them to the paper. Mark the date and newspaper where you found each ad.

4. Read the want ads from beginning to end. You may find jobs of interest in many different categories.

5. Analyze the ad. It's possible that you do not want the position because of the location, responsibilities, or other factors. Skip ads that require a degree, several years' experience, or travel. You would not qualify for those positions.

Responding to Classified Ads

When responding to ads, use the cover letter opening paragraph for classified ads shown in Chapter 6. If you fax the letter, enlarge the type to 12 or 14 points for clarity.

Recognizing the Key Words in Ads

Here is an example of a classified ad with the key words underlined. You would mention some of these words in the Skills section of your targeted resume and also in interviews.

> **Circulation Supervisor:** Entry-level, part-time position. Duties include <u>timely and accurate delivery</u> of the newspaper, route scheduling, <u>driver supervision. Assures completion of all routes</u>. Should demonstrate ability to <u>lead team</u> with <u>strong interpersonal skills</u>. Must have <u>truck or van</u>. Competitive salary and benefits. (555) 555-9999

This ad requires a telephone call for an appointment. Ask if you should send your resume beforehand or bring it with you.

Here's how to interpret the key words in the ad:

✉ **Timely and accurate delivery; assures completion of all routes.** The job probably starts at 4 a.m. You will deliver papers and be responsible for making sure the entire route is completed on time.

✉ **Driver supervision and lead team.** Your experience in playing sports or leading school committees would help you to supervise drivers and lead a team.

✉ **Strong interpersonal skills.** You will have to motivate and persuade your delivery people to do their jobs right.

✉ **Truck or van.** Do you have a truck or van to use every day? Feel comfortable asking if mileage and gas are reimbursed.

To Do:

Cut and paste four ads from the paper. (These can be any job ads and not the same ones you chose in Chapter 1.) Highlight or underline the key words in the ads.

Paste ad here

Paste ad here

Paste ad here

Paste ad here

List two skills or experiences that you think would be required for each of the four ads (for example, professional phone manner, dependable, sports experience, and writing).

Ad 1: _____

Ad 2: _____

Ad 3: _____

Ad 4: _____

Cold Calling

Cold calling takes a little bit of nerve, but it can pay off because you never know when a company will have an opening that suits you. Opportunities for cold calling are all around you. As you look around your town or neighborhood, do you see a company where you would like to work? Go into commercial buildings and read the directory of company names. Is there a company name that looks interesting? Look under the main headings in the yellow pages for companies of interest, too. You'll find many places to contact through cold calling.

Here are the steps for making a cold call in person. Take this list with you if you need to be reminded of what to do. You can turn this into a script to make cold calls by phone.

1. Open the main door to the company.

2. Talk to the receptionist and ask questions (even if the questions seem dumb).

3. Ask for or pick up a brochure on the company.

4. Ask if the company hires students for summer or part-time positions.

5. Ask how you can apply for a position.

6. Ask who you should see.

7. Ask for an appointment.

8. Ask if you can leave a resume for the hiring person.

9. Ask when you should call back.

Result: The receptionist will be impressed with your initiative and will remember you. If the receptionist looks annoyed, ask questions anyway and be very nice. When he or she gives your resume to the supervisor, the receptionist may comment on how inquiring and determined you were.

Using the Internet

The Internet is full of ways to find information about companies and jobs. You can look for industry topics, company names, product names, internships, and job openings.

Start with these search engines. Your library probably has Internet access, and your librarian can show you how to search for specific topics.

AltaVista	http://www.altavista.digital.com
Lycos	http://www.lycos.com
Yahoo	http://www.yahoo.com
WebCrawler	http://www.webcrawler.com

If you have an interest in eldercare, for example, you might want to work in an assisted living home, nursing home, or day care facility for the elderly for the summer. Type "Assisted Living" into the search engine. Many related Web page addresses and facility names will appear.

Click the pages that seem most relevant. Find facility names, their locations, and their contact information. Then call or write (either a letter or an e-mail) the ones in your area and ask about summer and part-time positions.

When you are searching Web sites, be sure to look for the names and e-mail addresses of managers or personnel directors. If you can find only the Webmaster's e-mail address, write and ask the Webmaster for the manager's e-mail address.

Cold Calling Worked for the Author

By luck and perseverance, I found my first job through cold calling when I was 17. I was looking for a job and was starting to feel discouraged and desperate. I was driving on a major highway and saw a large building. I drove over to the building, went in the door, saw the receptionist, and asked if the company was hiring secretaries (I could type very fast).

The receptionist said, "Yes," (wow!) and I set a time for the typing test. I left my resume for the hiring manager. In a week I went back, took the test, and was hired.

This is an example of an e-mail sent in search of an internship:

Subject line: Summer internship—high school senior

Dear Ms. Watkins:

I am interested in pursuing eldercare as a career and have visited your Web site. Your company's site is very impressive, and since I will be starting college in one year, I am interested in gaining experience as a student intern. It is my strong belief that my excellent communication skills, past experience working with senior citizens, and computer abilities would be a good match for your company.

Please e-mail me about your application process, as well as the proper person to contact regarding an internship, so that I can forward my resume for your consideration. Thank you for your time.

Sincerely,

Jen Grine

If you receive a positive response, send your resume by U.S. mail or e-mail. When sending a resume by e-mail, be sure to find out if the recipient can read attachments created in the word processing program you use. Instead of an e-mail attachment, you may have to send the resume inside the text box. If you're lucky enough to have a Web resume, refer the company your URL.

Good Web Sites for Your Job Search

For more information on job openings, resume writing, job search strategies, volunteer positions, community service opportunities, government educational programs, colleges, and leadership possibilities, visit these great Web sites. These sites were current at the time of publication.

Resume and Job Search Help

Student Center–http://www.studentcenter.com/. Start here for Internet research about jobs, career decisions, and resume writing.

The Monster Board–http://www.monster.com. One of the biggest job-related Web sites on the Net.

The Resume Place–http://www.resume-place.com. The author's Web site, which has tons of resume-writing information for high school students.

JIST Works–http://www.jist.com. The publisher's Web site, with free job-related book chapters, links to other career sites, and more.

Peterson's—http://www.petersons.com/. The Education & Career Center at this site offers information on careers, colleges, summer programs, and more.

State of New York Department of Labor—http://ny.jobsearch.org/winedge/samples.htm. This site has a page for high school students and contains important job search information.

Internships

Washington Post—http://www.washingtonpost.com/wp-adv/classifieds/careerpost/front.htm. *What Color Is Your Parachute?* author Dick Bolles has a page with a link to internships.

Summer Jobs

Cool Works—http://www.coolworks.com/. Links to more than 43,000 jobs in great places (ski resorts, ranches, cruise ships, National Parks). You have to visit this site! Check out what it takes to live and work in places that most people only visit.

Youth Conservation Corps—http://www.nps.gov/ccso/ycc.htm. YCC is a summer employment program for young men and women, ages 15 to 18, who work, learn, and earn together on projects that further the development and conservation of the natural resources of the U.S. The National Park Service operates YCC programs throughout the country.

Community Service and Service Learning Ideas

The Corporation for National Service—http:/www.cns.gov. Click on Learn & Serve. This program helps high school students gain workplace experience through a Congressionally chartered program.

School-to-Work Programs

School-to-Work—http://www.stw.ed.gov/general/whatis.htm. Good information on the new school-to-work program. This information can help you get a good job after you graduate.

Government Student Aid

The White House's Student Aid—http://www.whitehouse.gov/WH/Services/educate.html. Information on federal government student aid, scholarships, fellowships, internships, and agencies that sponsor young people's training and education programs.

College Search

U.S. News and World Report—http://www.usnews.com/usnews/edu/ college. Great college research site with answers to many questions about applying to and being accepted by colleges.

Careers

Spacezone—http://www.spacezone.com/edu/astroapp.html. Learn the qualifications to become an astronaut.

To Do:

Visit three of the Web sites listed. Write two sentences about what you learned at each site.

Web site 1: _____

_____

_____

_____

Web site 2: _____

_____

_____

_____

Web site 3: _____

_____

_____

_____

Find two more job-related Web sites that interest you and provide the following information.

Name of first Web site: _____

Web site address (URL): _____

Why is this Web site interesting to you? _____

_____

Name of second Web site: _____

Web site address (URL): _____

Why is this Web site interesting to you? _____

_____

Interview Tips from High School Students

So it's your big day. You have an appointment for an interview. Keep the following pointers in mind:

- ✉ **Dress nicely.** Wear nice clothes (but not jeans) that fit the company's image. You need to look like everyone there. If you don't know how to dress, go ahead of time and look at employees' clothes. If you're interviewing at a corporate office, for example, males should wear a sports coat, tie, and slacks. Females should wear a nice dress, stockings, and shoes with toes. Wear almost no jewelry, reasonable makeup, and a conservative hairstyle. If you're applying to a retailer like The Gap, you can wear good pants and a sweater that looks like a Gap sweater.

- ✉ **This is not the time to try a new deodorant.** Stick with what works, and be modest with your cologne or perfume. Some people are allergic to colognes.

- ✉ **Be confident.** If an employer hires you, he or she is getting a good employee, right? You'll help the company take care of customers, organize its store, or handle other important activities. You need to think positively.

- ✉ **Show up a few minutes early.** Don't get stressed out rushing, running, going through yellow lights, getting a speeding ticket, getting lost, and wrecking your outfit. Start early and stay calm.

- ✉ **Don't be afraid to make yourself sound great.** It's okay to say you're good at a few things. You are selling yourself. You want to get hired, right? Why should a company hire you? Because you can speak very comfortably with the public . . . because you're dependable and responsible . . . because you would like to get experience doing this work. An employer likes a person who knows his or her strengths. Memorize your list of strengths. Think of stories that will demonstrate your ability to do a good job.

129

- ✉ **Call at least a day ahead if you need to reschedule an interview.** It's okay to reschedule if something else very important comes up. Companies are usually accommodating if you give notice.

- ✉ **Keep your resume in an attractive folder** (not crumpled in your pocket). Go to an office supply store and buy a folder or portfolio to carry your resume and reference sheet.

- ✉ **Do not take backpacks, athletic bags, water bottles, books, or huge pocketbooks to an interview.** Keep it very light with a small folder or portfolio and a small purse (for girls).

- ✉ **Do not give your prospective employer an incomplete application or out-of-date resume.** Double-check your application. Update your resume before the interview so the interviewer does not have to ask questions that waste time. An interviewer will not appreciate your lack of consideration.

- ✉ **Bring a pen and notepad.** Take notes in the interview. You will need these notes for writing your thank-you letter. Be sure to get the correct spelling of the interviewer's name and his or her title. Get a business card if you can.

- ✉ **Ask questions.** Do research on the company before going to the interview. Find out how long it's been in business; how many employees it has; how many states it operates in; what its products or services are. Ask questions about the company's growth and goals. Employers appreciate the opportunity to answer questions instead of always asking questions. They will like your curiosity and interest.

- ✉ **Watch your posture, smile, and don't put your hands in your pockets.** Try to look sharp by standing up straight and looking friendly.

- ✉ **Be yourself** (unless you normally don't smile and have bad posture and atrocious manners). It's okay to be young and act young. The employer knows you're in high school and that you want experience and the chance to earn some dollars.

- ✉ **Keep eye contact with your interviewer.** Maintain eye contact with the interviewer when you are asked questions and give answers. This is very important.

- ✉ **Do not speak negatively of yourself or a former employer.** Skip all the bad history. Don't say that you left your last employer because the hours were too early, and you're not a morning person. Do not tell the interviewer that you did not get along with your last supervisor. Talk only about the good things. Interviewers are not impressed with anything negative. Stick with the positive about you and your experiences.

- ✉ **Do not bring food, drinks, or gum to an interview.** This is messy and absolutely not professional.

- ✉ **Be polite.** It's most important that you smile, have good manners, and say thank you after the interview.

Prepared Interview Notes

Be prepared before you go for an interview. Take extra resumes, bring your reference list, review your strong points, and jot down a few questions about the job, its responsibilities, and how it fits into the company. Try to find out whatever you can about a company, its products, and the job ahead of time. Good luck!

To Do:

List highlights of your education, experience, skills, and background to discuss in an interview. (Refer to your resume for help.)

Example: *I'm a high school junior looking for an administrative assistant position in international business, where speaking to customers in other languages is necessary.*

_____

_____

_____

_____

_____

_____

_____

Write your job-related strengths here and memorize this list.

_____

_____

_____

_____

_____

_____

_____

Write your answer to this interview question: "Tell me a little about yourself."

Example: *I am a junior at Lakeview High. My favorite courses are languages and history. My dad runs the family photography business and is an immigrant from Italy. I am used to foreign languages at home. I decided to take French throughout high school and will major in it in college. I'd like a job where I can use my knowledge of French.*

_____

_____

_____

_____

_____

_____

Write your answer to this interview question: "What can you offer my company?"

Example: *I am a hard worker and very responsible. I am fluent in French and speak two other languages somewhat. I understand business and customers from my family's business, and I can use computers quite well.*

_____

_____

_____

_____

_____

Index